In Pursuit of the Divine

WRITTEN STORIES TO EMPOWER A WOMAN'S SOUL

COMPILED BY

Krista Gustavson

In Pursuit of the Divine

ISBN: 978-0-9928173-4-3

Published in UK, Europe, US and Canada

Table of Contents

Thank You

I thank each one of my Inspiring co-authors from the bottom of my heart for having the courage to reveal their deepest truth and leap into creating this beautiful work of Art with me. Without this circle of women, this book would simply not have been born.

My parents for choosing to adopt me and my mom who always told me I could do anything I wanted in life, for giving me the freedom to explore who I was always.

Art & Terry Manville, my birth parents for bringing me into the world and for choosing me again. Sean Trotter for being my catalyst, inspiring the Feminine within me so I could align with my Vision. My three girls Ekiah, Elle and Emma who are my greatest teachers in the world for showing me who I am and for their love, patience and ongoing support while I created this Vision.

IN PURSUIT OF THE DIVINE

Introduction

In 2012 my soul spoke to me of collaboration being the most powerful and affective portal for supporting Women in business and working together as a collective. It has been a dream of mine to bring together a large group of Women in the Business of healing to co-create something extraordinary for the world! After two years of holding the Vision, my Anthology was placed before me. I did not have to think for a moment to know this was everything I had been dreaming. The co-creation of In Pursuit of the Divine became a gateway for empowering a woman's soul. As this circle of women came together and carved out our stories, several layers of healing were imminent, empowering the Feminine within us all again and again and again

Life stories represent who we are and reveal our true purpose. Every encounter, every relationship and every experience is our Soul's way of calling on us as a way to step up fully into our power and who we are in the world.

Within these 30 written stories, each co-author has a powerful message to share with you. All the little discoveries that led them to a deep inner wisdom, capturing the feminine essence of who they are. Each chapter will inspire the very depth of your soul.

Krista Gustavson

Krista Gustavson is the founder and director of Feminine Rising, the world's leading community and sanctuary for empowering a woman's soul. Krista's mission is to gather women all over the world to reclaim their feminine power and align with their true purpose so they can become the greatest expression of who they are. She is the creator of Your Story Reveals Your True Purpose. She is a Global leader, collaborator and co-creator for women all over the world who have a deep desire to cultivate healing with their offerings so that together we create massive transformations for our planet.

🏠 www.femininerisingretreat.com

📘 www.facebook/kristagustavson

🐦 www.twitter/kristagustavson

CHAPTER 1

Awakening My Soul's Purpose

By Krista Gustavson

❦

The angelic girl you are about to meet is often described as delicate, free- spirited, magical and mysterious. She has an unworldly power. Often I witness her petite body sprawled out in the middle of a dead end road soaking her skin on the hot pavement staring off into the great blue skies. It is here where she is dreaming of her future, a twinkle in her eye -not a care in the world. Then one day it all fell away, her dreams became shattered. It was 1974, only 4 years of her life on earth, a secret revealed, one that for any child would be difficult to grasp, something no mother could ever prepare her child for. The truth that was going to forever change her life and how she would show up in this world.

I was playing on the stairs, not a care in the world with my two older brothers as if this was the most natural way of exposing a child to a secret held deep in the heart of a mother. I heard her words, yet I only remember my answer. "So, what you're saying is, you are not my mother?"

In that fleeting moment I went off to play...

From that day forward my sweet essence, the little angel became completely flawed. Utter fear of rejection, insecurity and abandonment were imprinted on her soul.

Knowing I had been separated led me further and further away from my internal truth, the words in my mind revealed this to me "you're not enough" I built hard walls all around me to escape my own reality. I had grown up with a wonderful supportive family, I received everything I ever asked for, my mother so full of unconditional love yet I always yearned to know who I was, where I had come from, always felt disconnected, always curious, always contemplating and searching for home.

I was 16 years old, sitting at our dinner table. Every mortifying night was the same. I observed my mother speaking to me about someone I didn't know, except that she was speaking of me. Humiliation was piercing my heart, my walls closing around me a little more each time, the beliefs would become engraved in my mind. Her truth became mine. My voice cords transformed into that of a broken instrument, all expression of myself lost and forgotten, hidden deep within my soul, small and contained, a prisoner of my mind. Silence would become my second language, my body became my own sacred temple, the only place I could trust - and it was there that I would hide. It is there where I was safe.

Oct 2003 - It was only two months after I was married, living nestled in the country in our beautiful home with my family, 6 months pregnant with my third daughter, I received a peculiar phone call. My heart stopped for a fleeting moment. Could this be it? I listened intently to the message, these words spoke to me and she said "someone you are looking for is also looking for you". I sat in utter disbelief, I said to my husband, this is it... I paced for two hours with tears in my eyes looking deep within for the courage to begin this journey. My body trembled!

To my sweet surprise, I discovered something so magical, a moment I never could have imagined and that is when I'm certain time and space stood still.

The woman on the other end of the phone shared a story and this is what she told me. "Your birth parents are searching for you, they want to speak with you". oWhat, I stammered, they're married, how could this be?"

15

It was Heaven on Earth to discover the truth and all they must have endured to be married in the end. To this day, their partnership has become one of great Inspiration and hope, rare and precious.

I was told I had a sister and brother. Oh how I had always dreamed of having a sister and it was then that we immediately knew we were soul sisters, we became best friends.

Correspondence began the very next day. The first message came from my father. This is the man who would become my greatest mentor. As our relationships grew, I learned how to activate my inner wisdom. This new family, my catalyst for change. I became more aware of who I was, gently I opened my heart and spirit to my innate power. In 2005 the first seed to awakening whispered to me. I devoted myself to the Art of leadership with my mentor, my birth father as my guide. I was led to rediscovering and remembering who I am and my purpose on this earth. Each new experience of stepping outside of my limited beliefs would show me the way. I was a student of manifestation, my visions were guiding me to awakening my souls purpose but in the midst of all of this, a piece of my life came crashing down all around me.

I became a victim within my own marriage, abandoning my own children temporarily. Becoming a single mother was my new realty but it was this moment in time that empowered me to reconnect to my new self and who I had now become.

2010 - It was as if I was transcending in time and space, honoring my thoughts and feelings for the first time in my life with a burning desire to create. But my new family relationships tarnished, they faded away and the dark night of my soul was revealed to me. It was time to spread my wings and fly on my own to begin my passionate pursuit to the Divine. I witnessed another layer unfolding, a time to create something extraordinary for the world, but what could it be?

2012 - I took a risk. I had too much of this life, I felt so alone at first but then I embraced stillness and for over a year I sat in a state of unknowingness, connecting deeply with my inner self. I began to hear the whispers again asking me to create like I never had before. As my journey went on, it became clear, the healing of my old wounds hollering at me for love, attention, forgiveness. With this greater awareness as my guide, each of my wounds was showing me a gift, showing me the greatest expression of myself. In the shadows, every relationship awakening my senses, my greatest teachers in disguise. In pursuit of the Divine.

I was in a constant state of forgiveness, intrigued by my own freedom, my true purpose was now being revealed. I committed to always knowing and understanding that I had the answers for everything showing up in my life. I was devoted to my relationship with myself acknowledging my own truth but it wasn't found outside of me, it was deep within my heart and soul. It was here, the connection with myself where traces of knowledge were forming, rising fiercely from within me. It spoke to me of collaboration, co-creation and feminine leadership.

I knew in my heart i was being called to step up again to bring forth my innate inner wisdom. I witnessed my feminine power slowly open like a beautiful flower. Each new discovery, a spectacular thread in the tapestry to awakening my souls purpose. Boldly I declared my greatest vision for healing the planet.

My spiritual capacity increased, I became a dancer of the Divine. I felt the pulse of the universe, my soul was inspired. I was alive, I was free. I was daring to play bigger, I surrendered, I illuminated pure beauty. For two years I had an affair with my heart, it guided me closer and closer to remembering who I am. I embraced the portal between my fears and my dreams.

My own compelling story became my teacher. My deepest truth, my greatest expression gave me clarity around my purpose for healing our world. Today, it's the feminine within me, she speaks of the Feminine Rising, the world's leading community for empowering a woman's soul. A deep inner calling for sacred circles within a sanctuary, leading women with gentle guidance, compassion and fierce love in a safe container on their own inner journey to nourishing and healing the heart, in Pursuit of the Divine.

Your truth is not something you need to reach, find or create.
It is already vibrating fiercely in the depths of that which truly
matters to your soul.
– Chameli

IN PURSUIT OF THE DIVINE

Lisa Marie Rosati

Passionista and visionary, Lisa Marie Rosati is a renowned Inner Goddess Catalyst for women, Creatrix of The Goddess Lifestyle Plan and Sugar Free Goddess and co-author of the international bestselling book, *Embracing Your Authentic Self*. Lisa mentors women around the world on becoming a Modern Day Goddess. She teaches how to strategize and optimize key areas of life, so that women can experience a luscious goddess life overflowing with red-hot passion, vibrant health, entrepreneurial success, practical magic, sacred ritual, feminine mystery, spiritual connection and prosperity.

🏠 **Goddess Lifestyle Plan: www.goddesslifestyleplan.com**

🏠 **Sugar Free Goddess: www.sugarfreegoddess.com**

f **www.facebook.com/GoddessLifestylePlan**

🐦 **www.twitter.com/LisaMarieRosati**

📌 **www.pinterest.com/lisamarierosati**

in **www.linkedin.com/pub/lisa-marie-rosati/15/684/222**

CHAPTER 2

Modern Day Goddess

By Lisa Marie Rosati

છ૯જ૭

One of my core beliefs is: *life is magic.*

Today, I can voice that statement out loud with complete confidence and feminine strength. When you make the decision to look at life through a magical lens, life becomes a joyful, interesting and pleasure-filled adventure of EPIC proportions.

I know this because I live it… each and every day of my life.

But, that wasn't always the case.

My life has been filled with a lot of emotional pain, most of the suffering stemming from my feelings of not enough-ness, compounded by my empathic nature. This toxic, disempowering combination can cause one to make not-so-great choices most of the time. I was the sensitive soul who wanted so desperately to fit in, but wasn't desperate enough to conform. I was different from my family, much more eclectic and bohemian than all of them. They followed organized religion and I followed the moon cycles, my impulses and my folly – those behaviors were frowned upon. I look back and know, in my heart, that my parents were doing the best they could with the knowledge they had. I was, simply, a determined little girl that had absolutely NO desire to conform!

I ended up taking the long way around in life, and I'm finally at a place where I'm totally okay with it. As a matter of fact, my "mess" has become my message for women all over the globe. You see, my lovely, there's no right way to do life. We all just do the best we can with the information we've got at the time. My soul work in the world is helping women receive the essential information they need to create a magical, successful, empowered life and a lucrative business NOW!

My journey to the Divine was an unfolding of traumatic experiences that pushed me to my next level of enlightenment. Since my early twenties, I've worked towards integrating my spirituality with everyday life. And as I age and evolve, I realize that living my authentic truth, which is living magically and intentionally in the flow of nature and Universal Law, is an essential ingredient to my overall happiness, wellbeing and success in life and business. I've studied everything from Psychology to Hermetic Philosophy, and everything in between - including organized religions and their sacred texts. What was birthed out of those years of study, self-introspection and implementation of the teachings was the discovery that each woman has the capability of being a Modern Day Goddess.

Collectively, we recognize the inherent divinity in every being and every creature. Everything that's alive is, quite literally, the progeny of our Creator. We collectively speak of how everything is interconnected, that we are all one with Spirit and that every living creature has divinity within it. When I call myself a Goddess, I mean that statement *literally*.

I am the daughter of our Creator. I am a Goddess. And so are you.

While a Goddess possesses many wonderful characteristics and traits, I'm going to tell you the ones that together define my personal definition of a Modern Day Goddess. Let me introduce you to her.

A Modern Day Goddess is mortal, so she'll make her share of mistakes. However, she will embody most of the following characteristics, traits and mindsets, most of the time.

A Modern Day Goddess is:

A Creatrix – A Goddess is continually pregnant with possibilities and gives birth to her ideas and dreams. She will create her ideal life while living according to **her own** definition of happiness. She knows what she wants, sets fulfilling goals and has the courage to follow through in order to achieve her ultimate life vision.

Independent & Authentic – A Goddess doesn't seek approval in others, instead allows her intuition to guide her. She doesn't waste her time attempting to impress anyone because she knows her work, and the way that she lives her life speaks for itself.

Wildly Passionate – A Goddess exudes a *palpable* energy, authenticity and enthusiasm. Those qualities are attractive, contagious and inspiring. She's the woman in the room everyone gravitates to because she has that "certain something" that no one can put their finger on.

Always Evolving – A Goddess is continually learning and evolving. She is *always* putting her energy and focus towards working on her personal growth and becoming the greatest and most wise expression of herself.

Completely Congruent – A Goddess doesn't wear a false mask for the world because her public persona is the same as her innermost heart and soul; she is completely congruent.

Mindful To Take Care Of Her Body Temple With Self Love & Self Care – A Goddess is compassionate and forgiving with herself. She is fully aware that her body is her temple. She gets enough rest and gives her body the right fuel by deeply breathing in fresh air, eating correctly and drinking enough water. She knows what she needs to be at her best, and is sure to feed her body and her soul accordingly.

A Global Thinker & Environmentally Conscious – A Goddess is committed to the art of healing. She cares about **all aspects** that touch her and other people's lives. She works towards peace and understanding; whether on a large scale, or simply with her loved ones and closest circle of friends. She contributes to cleaning up the environment and encourages others to do so too.

Always Loving & Respectful Of Her Body – A Goddess views her body as sacred. She is comfortable with her sexuality, enjoys pleasure **in all its forms** without self- judgment, guilt or shame. She is directly connected to and in synch with the natural cycles of nature.

Patient & Balanced – A Goddess understands balance and patience; flow and ebb; waxing and waning. A Goddess doesn't stress or try to control ebb or waning times. Instead, she'll use the time and space

1996, a very sharp and intense pain woke me up. Hours later, I ended up in the hospital. Through all this, I was experiencing my spiritual breakthrough. I knew the answer to my prayers had been answered, and the Universe was giving me a taste of what I had been asking for.

The diagnosis was appendicitis, not a big deal, *right*? I wouldn't die from it. Long story short, they found a carcenoid (cancer) tumor throughout my entire appendix. If I didn't have appendicitis this cancerous tumor would have reached my colon, small intestine, major organs and silently killed me.

To everyone's surprise, I had been naturally and homeopathically raised, and was an athlete, nature lover, good eater, good student and a visionary. Everyone questioned the doctors on why and how this could happen to me? I knew why. I knew, deep in my soul and heart, that my demands had been answered, and this disease was created by me. Yes, you are hearing correctly. I created my own tumor; I asked for death and it was on its way, silently.

At 15 years old, I refused major surgery. I knew I had created this reality and took responsibility for my own actions. I became aware that the Universe was telling me something and it was up to me to listen and take action.

I had been given a second chance to live.

For six months, I went through a holistic body cleanse and homeopathic regiment. Six months later, I was clear and in love with life. I had been given a second chance. I am proof that our mind, heart and soul create either a healthy or sick body. I am proof that the Universe won't give up on us if we don't give up on ourselves. I am proof that I am creator of my own reality.

For years, I was truly happy, in peace, in love and in discovery of my inner Goddess. I didn't know my life's purpose yet, but I was getting there. By living with AWARENESS, APPRECIATION, GRATITUDE AND LOVE – I'd healed it all.

Just when I thought I had it, I fell deeper into the abyss. This time I became the victim and the abuser.

August 1999 started the second chapter of my Goddess discovery. That year, we moved to the USA—my mom had finally left my dad, after 25 years of marriage.

August 2001, I met my daughter's father. I was in love with his eyes, soul, Italian heritage, inner child-like innocence and desire to be loved (love was something I had a lot of to offer). But I was in denial of all our differences. I had just reentered the vicious cycle that I had refused to ever experience again.

Abuse isn't only what you receive from others, it's also what you allow to be inflicted and what you stop doing for yourself.

I had lost my identity, my sacred meditation temple, my spiritual practice and my self-love. As a result, I steered away from finding my life's purpose. I had no purpose and no clue. Instead, I focused on being the perfect daughter, sister, housewife, employee and friend. But in reality, I was keeping myself busy because I was empty and craving appreciation, gratitude, freedom, peace and unconditional love.

At the beginning, my husband wasn't abusive. During disagreements, he would lock himself in his room; this made me furious because I felt alone and ignored, all the more. I became bitter and resentful. I lost myself in the feeling of entitlement; and over time, I became the abuser of him and myself. We had learned to push each other's buttons. I wanted to leave, but I couldn't; I was afraid.

Abuse is addictive. You think you won't make it, you feel isolated and you cannot see the light at the end of the tunnel. This vicious cycle was repeating itself; something I swore as a child to break free from. We became emotionally, psychologically and physically abusive to each other. We were living on the rollercoaster of abuse.

I got pregnant. We were not trying to, but I had hoped things would get better. They didn't. Our life was going downhill. He had lost his job, twice, and I had lost mine before my daughter turned four weeks old. We tried to work things out for our daughter's sake; we did school together, traveled, volunteered, opened a business and logged countless hours of family time. We were finally on the same page; I thought we had made it.

Did we?

Kids are a true reflection of their parents and home environment. Let's stop denying it and accept that truth.

As a toddler, our daughter had a mind of her own, and knew what she wanted. On play dates, a lot of the times, she would push, hit or bite other children. I was mortified; I thought my daughter was possessed! I knew things had to change immediately. I blamed her dad for the vicious, karmic abuse she had inherited. We tried several marriage counselors, with no luck. Then, my spiritual mentor told me, "your daughter is not the one who is all over the place; it's you!" She was right because children are a direct reflection of our own inner being.

I was all over the place with my mind, emotions and soul. This truth was reflected in my daughter's behavior and interaction with other kids. If my daughter was angry or yelling to get attention, it was because she was a reflection of my and her father's interactions.

While I was getting my Reiki certification, I began to see clearer than ever. No matter what I was doing—and lying to myself about—my daughter was living the same vicious cycle I had lived as a child. I knew I was the only one who could break the cycle and liberate her from this path.

Right away, I asked for a divorce and left the house with no possessions. I was reclaiming our freedom by detaching myself from all the material things I left behind. My husband claimed that I was breaking our family apart. I reasserted that I was liberating our family. He stated that marriage was forever. I stated that family is forever.

We both knew it was the best thing to do, but he was in denial and I was still afraid of failure. We knew we would still love each other forever because we'd been there for one another when others hadn't. We knew these vicious, abusive cycles took a lot out of us, and that we had intense personal growth work ahead, if our daughter was to truly inherit freedom.

Our relationship didn't work out; but after years of ups and downs, we had developed awareness, appreciation, gratitude and love for each other and our surroundings. We have become the best friends I had never thought possible.

Let's focus on the positive that arises from the negative, and we will welcome awareness, appreciation, gratitude and love.

What has been working for us?

We've become more aware, and appreciate the great lessons we have learned from our former relationship. We now take responsibility of our own flaws. I am an abuser; but by being aware of it, I've stopped by changing my actions and thoughts.

Awareness opens your heart to appreciation, gratitude and love. It's the beginning of acceptance, which perpetuates change. Through awareness, I've awakened my inner Goddess.

Liberate your Inner Beauty at www.LiberatingInnerBeauty.com

Experience Transformation and Empowerment at www.BH-BB.com

Rachel Harris, ART, BSc (Hons)

Rachel Harris is an intuitive healer, certified medium and spiritual coach/channel who shares her journey of reconnecting to Spirit and her authentic gifts of intuition, clairvoyance and healing. Her soul remained resilient, even when the rest of her gave up. As a result, she healed and transformed her life through remembering her mystical gifts and connecting with the Divine.

She guides people to reconnect to their soul and Spirit, and passes along loving messages and healing from angels, guides, departed loved ones, Archangels and Ascended Masters. She teaches her *Bright Shiny Soul* program and loves watching students transform their lives and their stories.

📞 + 1 (604) 928 3420

✉️ info@rachelintuitivehealer.com

🏠 www.rachelintuitivehealer.com

f www.facebook.com/rachel.harris.3367

CHAPTER 4

Bright Shiny Soul
– At Last!

By Rachel Harris, ATP, BSc (Hons)

❦☙❦

My Soul never gave up even when the rest of me did. As the fabric of my life finally tore apart and I fell through, something caught me. An angel. Love. Me. I just didn't recognize it yet.

My childhood was idyllic. I lived in a lovely English home near the sea with my lovely mum and dad – and a brother, who was occasionally lovely! All was perfect.

Then, one evening when I was seven, all that changed.

I was upstairs watching my mum getting ready to go out. My legs were swinging off the end of the bed as she was applying her makeup. I looked around and noticed a photo of my mum pushing my brother, Mike, in a toy cart.

"Mummy, how old is Mike in this photo?"

With mascara wand in hand, she peered over. "About four." she replied.

My little brain furiously tried to work out the math. "Mummy, does that mean I was in there?" I pointed to her tummy.

She looked at me. "No darling, you weren't in there. You were adopted. Your mummy couldn't look after you the way she wanted you to be looked after, so she gave you to daddy and me to look after, and we love you so very much."

Although I didn't think too much about it at the time, from that day forward, a story began in my head that went something like, *why didn't my mummy want me; what's wrong with me?* As I grew, it grew with me. It grew bigger than me. It became my perspective on all of life. I thought, *wow, if my own mum didn't want me, what does that make me?*

At times, I felt worthless, unlovable and rejected. No one actually said anything like that to me; my mum and dad loved me, unconditionally. My ego had made the whole thing up and fear had me in its grip.

But my soul never gave up.

As I was growing up, a rather curious thing happened. With my ego's massive victim story running amok, my Spirit was ignited, and seeking my attention to pull myself from darkness into light. I was about four when I had my first mystical experience—a gentle brush on the cheek would awake me from a repetitive nightmare. Later, established religion and "the Jesus thing" held my attention for a while.

At age 20, I moved to London and shared an apartment with a family friend. It was as if the Universe had conspired: "Pssst, she's out of her family home – let's go take a visit." I was seeing and hearing things that were far from ordinary. I could hear voices at night and see shadows and colors creep across my bedroom. Eventually, fear won and I cried, "Enough! I don't want anything to do with this – and you, God, whoever you are, I don't want anything to do with you either."

I shut it all out, and lived a very "normal" life for about ten years. I was holding back that deeply intimate, spiritual part of myself with all its mystical and wonderful wisdom. I had forgotten to be all of me.

The Divine tried many times to remind me, but I ignored it. Finally, I was shocked into remembering. At the age of 34, my brother took his own life. I cannot imagine the despair or courage he must have had to stand, wait and be hit by that train. *What the hell must have gone through his mind?*

My mum, dad and I carried the guilt of being unable to stop this tragedy. We tormented ourselves. Occasionally, we would share; but mostly, we carried our guilt alone.

The fabric of my life finally tore, and I fell through. I drank to numb physical pain that was a constant companion in my stomach; and I drank to be able to talk about Mike. I recall putting a knife to my wrist and wondering whether, if he couldn't make it through life, perhaps I couldn't either. Like me, he was adopted; maybe, he, too, felt worthless and unlovable. I was angry with him for doing what he had done to us. The anger masked my deepest fear of being abandoned because I wasn't worthy enough of his love. Just like my birth mother, he had left me. In that moment, I felt like giving up, but Spirit reached out. An invisible force within me put the knife calmly down.

I stumbled along, sometimes crawling, with grief and my old demon of being worthless as constant companions. Finally, Spirit reached me and gifted me a miracle.

When a friend (as many had before) suggested I speak with a counselor, I heard the advice as if for the first time. Within about a week, I found myself at my doctor's clinic for a routine appointment. As I was waiting, I noticed a poster on the door. "Have you recently lost someone?" it read. *Yes,* I thought. "Are you finding it difficult to cope?" *Yes.* The poster seemed to grow in front of my face: "Call a bereavement counselor today...."

I eagerly took the number down. I just knew I had to call, and Bella became my bereavement counselor for several years. She was my guide as I began to mend the fabric of my life.

Slowly, I began to heal and hear my Soul's whispers. Eventually, I trusted my intuition enough to make a dream come true. My husband and I left everything we knew and set off on a travel adventure and to a new homeland. Our first stop, for several months, was Africa. Africa awakened me, *literally.*

I was sitting in the dirt on the ground in Malawi outside our tent. My dear friend Suzie had some 'Angel cards'.

"What are they?" I asked.

"Divination cards, like Tarot but with Angels. Here, have one."

I took one, and a deep shiver went from the top of my head down my back. I took another one, and the same thing happened. I looked at her and stammered "I don't know how I know about these 'Angels', but I know all about them."

And that was it. I awoke, remembering all my "weird" gifts and the spiritual encounters I had experienced as a child. There was no turning back. My Soul had finally reached me, and I joyfully reconnected to it and the Divine.

After months of travelling, we arrived in Canada. It was a fresh start, and I felt like I could be anything I wanted to be! I devoured everything spiritual that crossed my path. It was the angels who spoke loudest to me; and I connected to them daily, trusting their messages and my intuition. I couldn't believe I had made up a story that had impacted my life for so long.

It took forty years, but I was finally ready to reach out to find my birth mum. It felt like a dream as things just slotted into place.

This was the hardest letter I had ever written. I didn't know if she was alive or even what to call her. Should I write *Dear Mum* or *Dear Sally*? What if she rejected me, *again*? Thankfully, I gave up and let Spirit take over. I chose love, and it flowed straight from my heart.

Within a month of my sending that letter, I found myself at an English castle in the warm embrace of my mother. In that moment when we held each other, she was shaking from head to foot, and I really understood how much she had longed to hold her daughter again. She loved me, and had always loved me. She had been 21, unmarried and living at home. Her mother wouldn't let her keep me. Instead of being worthless to her, she loved me so much that she gave away her most precious gift.

We have an incredible relationship. It's forgiving, grateful, honest and spiritual. I'm so excited to have a new sister, niece and nephew! Through her trust and connection to the Divine, she also chose love. All along, she had openly talked about me and kept photos of me. This allowed for an easy and loving reunion.

Finally, there is a new fabric to my life, one of love, joy and oneness with the Divine. Spirit, "synchronicity", my intuition and "team" of angels and guides showed me I could choose Love and Spirit over fear

35

and ego. I am deeply grateful for my journey however painful and dark the shadows are at times. Through this journey, I found the gift and freedom to be all of me. Now, my soul shines brightly far more often.

My soul never gave up; and thank God for that, given all the adults and children Spirit inspires and heals through it. I am a mother of two young boys and I teach them tools to reconnect with Spirit. I also have a thriving business using my gifts, intuition and clairvoyance to guide and heal adults and children. I pass along loving messages and healing from their "team" of angels, guides, departed loved ones, Archangels, and Ascended Masters.

I love teaching *Your Bright Shiny Soul Program*, and watching people transform their stories and lives. Their true selves are revealed and miracles attracted as they connect to Divine love.

They too shine brightly.

Melissa C. Waldron

Melissa helps spirit-conscious entrepreneurs step into their "blue flame" with passion and purpose, while co-creating a larger vision for themselves and expanding their impact on the planet. As an intuitive business guide, she helps her clients create unique tribe-building and engagement strategies that come from a place of authenticity at the soul level. While supporting and nurturing clients, Melissa helps them navigate their way towards becoming their future self. She encourages them to align with their soul-purpose mission and step into a life of fulfillment and prosperity, while making a difference on the planet.

📞 **(646) 408-9653**

✉ **melissa@redhotnow.com**

🏠 **www.redhotnow.com**

f **www.facebook.com/RedHotNow**

CHAPTER 5

Believing the Tether is There

By Melissa C. Waldron

ᕙᖴᗜᕋ

You know that feeling of inertia from being stuck in a project, and that feeling of inertia turning into cement? That was me, a few years ago. But what had stalled was more than a project. It was my life.

I was the contributing producer for a public radio food series, and I also ran a small boutique marketing business for sustainable food products. I had the pleasure of writing about local food producers and farmers for magazines and websites. My husband was a cinematographer. We owned a tiny apartment in Brooklyn Heights and a condo in Connecticut.

On the outside, life seemed good. But inside, there were rumblings, whispers and the restlessness of spirit.

There is something bewitching about New Mexico. The expanse of desert and limitless sky, combined with crisp air, is intoxicating. One birthday, I spent an evening alone in an iron, hot springs, mineral pool, nestled in its northern mountains. A bright, crisp, white crescent moon shone above, calling me to take notice of the moment. Perhaps the hours of hot mineral waters had taken their toll but something in me had shifted. I felt open.

In the wind, I could hear my mother's voice. She was asking me a question. *What happens now?* My mother was right. What was I doing with my life? I didn't even have to think, my inner guidance took over and the answer came forth.

"Ok mom, no more bullshit." I said out loud. No more avoiding, no more pretending. It was time to let go.

My mother's death, only a few years before then, had become my own story. I was hiding in her shadow and avoiding the onerous task of taking total responsibility for my own life. The victim persisted. I did not want to hear what Spirit had to say. I did not want to grow up and step into my own power. But here amongst the copper, iron-coated stones with steam rising around my head in tranquil healing water, I decided to turn that ship around. Her death was to become a great gift—a gift that would allow me to follow my own path, my own heart. This is a story of a mother's gift to a daughter.

It was time to answer the questions of a lifetime. *What would life be like if I let go of my old story? Who would I become?* And so the quest began.

If my life were a river, I would have been swimming maniacally upstream, scrambling to find a rope to the riverbanks, a tether, to prevent the currents of anxiety from carrying me away in its undertow. Anxiety is separation from self. It was time to trust that the tether was there, the inner knowing that a richer, fuller life awaited me. I would finally allow the connection to flourish between the woman who was, the woman who is and the woman who would be. I wanted to swim downstream.

I am a recovering WASP, but there is no twelve-step program; it's DIY. I grew up amongst the mansions of Fortune 500 CEOs in the 1980s— stifling Reagan-esque consciousness of social status that inhabited the North Shore of Chicago—but our household was not the average Lake Forest home. My mother, Nancy Waldron, was a psychic.

Mom was very "tapped in" and people often visited us for a reading. She drew people's auras with water color pencils. She read palms. She wrote reams of poetry, supposedly, channeled by guardian angels. Often she told me to ask her angels for help but I would just roll my eyes. By the age of 16, I thought it was just airy-fairy-woo-woo crap.

Ours was a relationship born of frustration. It was clear we were here together to push each other's buttons. My mother always told me; from birth she knew I was a "spitfire." I didn't let her down.

My mother, the psychic. It was a novelty growing up. When I was a child, she used the Oujia board and levitated the kitchen table with the touch of her fingertips. Ash trays moved. Lights flickered on and off. And ghost stories were daily chit-chat. Mom often saw dead people.

My early childhood tether was the ghosts my mother promised me.

Sometimes I saw ghosts too. Wilma was my friend and confidant. We had tea together under the backyard willow tree. Only I could see her. Wilma was my maternal grandmother, killed in a car accident when mom was only 16 years old. Wilma watches over me today; although, I stopped "seeing" her around the age of six.

My mother never recovered. Steeped in grief, in a fine patina of ever greying sorrow, Mom's way of relating to me — her only child — was by sharing that grief through ever-growing histrionics, dramatic outbursts of anger and anxiety-ridden depression. I bathed in her anguish my whole childhood, knowing the only way to get through it was to be in solidarity with her. If I was depressed, she was happy. My father, a dutiful husband and former advertising-executive-turned-realtor who looked dapper in Brooks Brothers suits, was at his best when talking about mortgage rates and property tax; but was terrified of all the unleashed emotion that flew around the house. He sank into his own depression as I was growing up.

My parents were too absorbed by their own ghosts to take notice of me. I was the girl who was best seen but not heard.

Nature was my tether growing up. Running through cornfields, exploring the woods, climbing gingko trees and riding horses was where my spirit soared. Occasionally, I would wander around the woods pretending to be Helen Keller, my childhood hero. With eyes closed, I stumbled and fell but never gave up until I found the gravel path underneath my feet. I remember hearing my dad call my name for dinner; but since I was "mute", I couldn't respond. I kept walking. I got in trouble that day for "disappearing" but knew I was happier getting lost than being found.

Disappearing became my favorite pastime. Becoming invisible. The pain of being seen was too much to bear.

Luckily, I did get seen when I was two days old; by a doctor who discovered that I had hip dysplasia, which is another way of saying my thighbones and pelvis were not connected. I technically had no hips. The physical grounding in my life, my root chakra, my tether to this earth was disconnected coming into this world. That's when the defiance began. The renegade was born. OH YES I AM became my mantra.

This defiance carried me a long way. It became my champion and brought me to New York City to be in the world of documentary filmmaking, so I could tell the story of the underdog. I needed to fight for those who could not fight for themselves. Whether producing PBS political news shows or educational films, I was their protector. And I was fierce.

Defiance led me into the world of sustainable agriculture. Producing the food radio show taught me about the challenges of industrial agriculture and to not accept the status quo. I dedicated myself to learning about local food systems, and I received an urban farm training certificate from Growing Power in Milwaukee. I moved from NYC to New Haven, Connecticut with the intention of creating urban farms while getting reconnected to the land, and buying a house with a backyard garden that one day would become an experiential learning center for children.

My tether today is the act of coming home to myself, by letting go of constructs I thought to be true and trusting something deeper. I am enough, and more. Through this daily practice, I have been able to gather the courage to declare my own intuitive abilities and go after my dream of becoming an entrepreneur from a place of purpose and passion, and following my heart's desire and soul's purpose of helping others produce businesses that are healing to the planet.

I am a Visionary Business Producer. But, we must heal ourselves first. Self-love is the essential ingredient for healing to occur.

Entrepreneurism is a spiritual act, one that can lead us to peace and prosperity. But we must first listen to and trust our own voice. That is Spirit speaking. Then, we must commit. By deciding to

41

commit unconditionally, with no turning back, is how we find true fulfillment—a treasure richer than money can buy.

The negative childhood beliefs you constructed are powerful. However, they are not impenetrable. If you think they are like concrete, get a jackhammer. The only belief that you need to keep and nourish is the belief in yourself that anything is possible. Believe that you are the connection—the tether—to Spirit. That is my wish for you.

Reverend Katherine McClelland, MA

The main ingredients of Katherine's unique philosophy and method are embodied soul and practical tools for self-love; grounded and aligned in our body, mind, heart and soul. She helps women claim their sexiness and vitality, while creating their wildest dreams in their career or personal lives.

Before her career as a Soulful motivational speaker and Model & Beauty and Visibility Specialist, she worked as a business woman, a Body Awareness and Relationship Coach, Transformational Leadership Facilitator, spiritual leader, movement instructor, nutritional advisor and mother. Katherine holds an M.A in Spiritual Psychology, a B.A. in Psychology and is an Ordained Minister.

- KatherineMcClelland.com
- Discovery Page: KatherineMcClelland.com/discovery
- www.facebook.com/katherine.mcclelland.18
- www.facebook.com/pages/Raw-Naked-Beauty-Project
- www.facebook.com/katherinemcclellandembodiedwisdom

CHAPTER 6

Raw Naked Beauty

By Reverend Katherine McClelland, MA

୧୬୬୬

My life has been beautiful, unusual, dramatic, traumatic, powerful and blessed.

My life, from the beginning, grew into a crescendo of separation and distance from the feminine; and from there, it was years in the unfolding of my transformation home. At many different times, it seemed that my light might have gone out forever. I did not have just one dark night of the soul, but many. I seemed to progress through all the gates needing to find my way in each arena. Finally, I have put together all the pieces—heart, mind, body and soul—and am living in the balanced feminine love field with the masculine in powerful service to my heart, dreams and desires, for myself, humanity and the Universe.

I was born in the Saudi Arabian desert in a sleepy little American consulate outpost in Dhahran. I was one of five children and one of two twin girls. I spent most of my life in the Middle East, moving from place to place; from Saudi Arabia to Lebanon to Iraq to Iran to Kuwait in and out of America twice and finally to Egypt. It was the beginning of what turned out to be a life that sometimes had a glamorous and prestigious façade, but was full of the darkness of the wounded masculine and the strangulation or dismissal of the feminine.

In Lebanon, my blond hair was cut to keep men from grabbing me in the streets. In Iraq, where tensions were high and war and insurrection were common, we were in a constant state of high alert. Within me,

I was able to maintain my childhood, dancing and playing; but then, at six years old everything changed. We were evacuated from Iraq under the cover of darkness in the most dangerous of moments and circumstances. Women and children alone crossed the desert in the middle of the night. We got out safely with one tiny suitcase, but I lost everything else; and with it, a piece of my little girl and her heart.

Up to that point in my life, most of the threat to me had been outside of my home. But when I came to live in America, for the fist time, it came from the inside. My mother went back to work and left us under the supervision of an unfortunate cadre of misfits and malevolent characters, some of whom were "family friends".

Between the ages of eight and ten, I experienced various types of sexual abuse and molestation at the hands of a babysitter. Having escaped from him, upon my arrival in Kuwait, I encountered more of the same from a cook who would touch me in our kitchen and share pornographic pictures with me in his quarters behind our house. The trauma of these years left their mark on me. I felt the effects of the powerful and dominant masculine, and had no place to hide. I began to turn deeply within and bury the precious young girl.

From Kuwait, where terrorism became the new worry, to the United States and the culture shock of a toxic urban high school, I existed in environments that continued to become more dangerous and harsh. I began avoiding school and almost failed tenth grade, spending as much time as possible in the theater with the hidden feminine as my only lifeline.

Through college into my twenties, I experienced more disassociation from the feminine. I was raped and never spoke of it. I did not have the ability to stand up for myself. However, I did well in school. I chose to prove myself as an intellectual to hide any kind of femininity. Leaving the theater behind, I put the feminine to sleep, allowing her to rest below the surface of my intelligence and competence in the world.

Upon graduation from college and through my first few jobs, I landed in New York City. Intensely driven and competent, I relied on the power of the masculine in my life. My job was hard and harsh—60+ hours, six days a week. I began to feel depleted from living this driven and demanding life. I had worked hard and gotten the job of my dreams, but it was empty, lonely, dark and filled with unethical and uncaring behavior.

At this point, I was completely separated from my femininity, my power, the feminine energy that lifted and loved through me. I began considering suicide. Without knowing, I had already killed my spirit. I was worried that my body would have to follow. I was desperate for change. All I had was me, and the way I was living left me angry, lonely, hurting, empty and afraid. Something had to give.

The Transformation Begins:

When I was 27, I was gifted a seminar by my twin sister, who had been quite worried about me. As my heart opened, I began to find my way home to myself. After years of neglect, separation from my identity and the feminine and years of pain and trauma, I slowly learned to trust, love and care passionately. I left my work, volunteered for the seminars and waitressed to live. I even cried, for the first time since I was seven years old.

After being quickly married and divorced in my early 30s, the deeper, psycho-spiritual realms began to call me. Combining the teachings of spirituality and psychology, I earned a MA degree. I was lifted into a realm that gave me tools and a sense of internal safety.

At 40—in the midst of my second marriage with three children to care for—I was devastated by the death of my twin sister and the loss of trust in my husband. I entered into inner darkness once again. Yearning still for something I had not found, this time I ventured into the ministry. I studied, preached and taught for eight years as a minister of a universal spirituality. Opening into this deeper spiritual realm, I found safety in meditation, compassion and kindness. This began my awakening to the feminine realms within.

My heart was open, my mind was aligned, my Spirit began to be nurtured in the feminine, and then my body fell apart. I had not been able to bring the qualities of the feminine, which were nurturing me from within, into everyday life. I was still struggling with relationships, partnerships and parenting. All of the anger, hurt and trauma from my past had seeped into my life again, and was now showing up in my body. I severely broke my wrist, and within five years had five surgeries. My marriage was falling apart, and I was burnt out from a ministry of giving too much. I began the search of finding my way back into a loving relationship with my body.

During the time I was contemplating leaving my marriage, I had three abnormal cell tests. Just after I left and began standing for the internal power I needed to express, all three: cervical, vaginal and breast biopsies came back clear! I was on my way.

Over the next couple of years, the trauma of my divorce highlighted my need to change my relationship with my body forever. Overweight with health issues and toxic stress, I started to gather my body in the love I was yearning for. I began to feel pleasure, enjoy my life and allow myself to be seen and fully valued as a woman.

Finally into my body, I brought what I had in my mind, heart and soul. It was a feminine, gentle, loving approach; a healing spirituality of love. I could no longer maintain the master/slave, masculine-overlord of self-abuse as I had in the past. This journey was to be a pleasurable, gentle and loving relationship of awareness with myself and my body. I needed some good solid education and practices of nutrition, movement, body awareness and yoga in order to create my very own body of love.

Rebalancing My Life with Alignment in My Heart:

I allow myself to flow with life—to feel, to express, to give, to receive, with a wholehearted openness. I allow my heart to be broken open. I stand firmly and with great power as an able woman, cheetah, lioness. I'm both gentle and soft until something needs to be protected. And now I can. I am the flexible openness that I want to be.

And finally as a bonus, the beauty I have always yearned for lives within me each day as love, passion and understanding. Through a gentle alignment of body, mind, heart and soul, and a balance of feminine and masculine energies, I allow myself to show up each day whole, healthy, powerfully gentle and inspiring. I have an inner radiance that allows me to shine from the inside out. I am grateful, raw, naked and beautiful.

Sandy Dow

Sandy Dow believes in a world where people converse with the trees, dance bare foot, and treasure small moments. Sandy's journey has formed her love of play, and her strengths as a healer, visionary, and intuitive. Years of study and client work in Shamanism and Somatic Based Therapy inspires the depth and unique style of her coaching. Her expertise attracts people in high-stress situations who hunger to achieve their full professional potential. As a teacher and mentor, she shares her talents for weaving ancient spiritual practices into our modern day world, and empowers others to be unstoppable.

- www.sandydow.com
- thedows@telus.net
- www.facebook.com/SandyRDow1?ref=br_rs
- www.twitter.com/visions11

CHAPTER 7

Dancing Through the Storms

By Sandy Dow

From as far back as I can remember, I was afraid of almost everyone and everything. As a child, I was so shy and sensitive that you would find me hiding in the closet when company dropped by, and crying inconsolably when a tree was chopped down. I was an only child, had a mother who worked fulltime, and lived in a house that was full of tension and fear whenever my dad was home.

My anxiety and loneliness became even more overwhelming when I awoke, one morning when I was five, to find my all of my dad's belongings missing. He had left. Confused and devastated, I ran into my mother's arms and we cried together. As I tried to make sense of this new reality, I felt myself withdrawing deeper into my shell.

Through all of this chaos, my mom was my rock. I knew she was making every sacrifice she could to provide a better life for me. The two of us, and our beloved cat, were now a family. I began to find peace spending hours buried under a pile of library books or alone in the woods across the street from my house.

Whenever I visited the forest, the shyness would fade and my spirited self would come out of hiding. Here, I would sing to the trees and dance for the birds. I found this magical landscape enchanting; it provided a safe and comforting contrast to the disconnection I felt around people.

Nature seemed to speak a language I could understand and speak more fluently than my own. This was where I felt at home.

As a teenager, my struggle with anxiety continued. But even though my withdrawn and introverted ways cloaked me like a heavy blanket, my inner essence was very much alive. I had fierce passions that would draw me out into the world, and I found myself combating fears to advocate for causes that supported the environment and mistreated animals. I had always loved music and dance lessons until a recital was scheduled. Even though I could muster the courage to be in the spotlight, I would be ill and anxiety-ridden for days before a performance.

Over the years, the fragile relationship with my dad was slowly being rebuilt. But when I was sixteen, this tenuous connection was shattered when his life ended from illness at the age of forty. Shattered by emotions and grief, I could again feel a part of me disappearing inside. Though my heart had been torn apart, my strong spirit and mother's unyielding support, helped me keep moving forward.

Years passed, and I gratefully found my way into an adult life that was full and abundant. By my thirties, I was married, had a house, three children, and a fast-paced job at a local hospital. I was thankful for the nurturing and grounding that family life gave me. But, the internal stress and anxiety was always present. In my late thirties, I found a way to deflect from these emotions by taking on physical challenges. I decided to turn my casual jogging into running a marathon, and then went on to endure several more years of pushing my body to its limit to achieve a black belt in karate.

Although both of these were huge accomplishments, my body, emotions and spirit were becoming worn and depleted. Nagging ailments were now erupting into endometriosis, heart palpitations, chest pain and a burning skin rash. I felt disconnected from my children, my marriage was failing and my job was feeling toxic. There was something that I had to face within myself, and I had been ignoring the signals for too long.

I knew the first step would be quitting my job. I had worked at the hospital for 25 years, and the tragedy and heartbreak I had witnessed in that period had left a toll on me. I also developed an acute sense that there was more to healing than western medicine could address. But I hesitated, overwhelmed with fear at the thought of taking this massive step. However, one night my body spoke more clearly, shocking me awake with crushing chest pain that I could no longer ignore. I quit the next day.

I was now free to search for help for my health issues. I was frantic to find alternate ways of supporting my body in recovery, but this was an unfamiliar landscape to me. I had no roadmap to follow. Then one day, in a moment of darkness and exhaustion, I surrendered my search and prayed to be shown a way forward. Miraculously, within a matter of days, I was shocked when several friends unexpectedly provided information that led me to a variety of modalities and practitioners. I then nervously stepped into the hands of a Shamanic healer, an acupuncturist, and the consciousness based holistic method of Bodytalk.

I began to learn about the relationship between my emotions, stress and illness. I was amazed at how these powerful, yet gentle, treatments contributed to vast improvements in my heath; despite being told that surgery and medication were the only options available to me. At this time, with my hope and strength returning, I found myself led one more time, to a shamanic drumming circle. During a sacred ceremony, I was introduced to my spirit animal, and I was stunned. These ancient teachings were speaking the language I recognized from my childhood in the forest. I was hungry to learn more, and apprehensively, I embarked into a two year Shamanic apprenticeship.

Here I fell completely in love with the compelling indigenous practices. This new horizon offered a breath of life to my beleaguered emotions and spirit. My relationship with my husband had deteriorated greatly over this time, and beautifully, this had now provided an unexpected foundation for the healing of my marriage.

Shamanic training, however, was by no means for the faint of heart. One of my biggest trials would be a vision quest; where I spent several days fasting, alone in the forest. Here I endured freezing temperatures, aching bones from unyielding ground, and the punishing fears the aloneness created in my mind. This was an ultimate test of my endurance emotionally and physically. Remarkably, by the last day, with my tortured mind finally silent, I found myself on the other side of that darkness. I woke up to an indescribable sensation of inner peace that granted me a sense of the profound wisdom that can be accessed in stillness.

Many more initiations and Shamanic teachers later, I now felt eager to share what I had learned and started my own healing practice. With an avid passion for young people, I began to host drum circles in my home and at a recovery house for adolescent girls where I was working. Here I witnessed first-hand how hungry young people are for spiritual wisdom. I was constantly amazed at how naturally they understood that there is much more to our world than we can see or understand with our rational minds. The Shamanic teaching circles and the bonds created from these gatherings, helped encourage this group to form their own community of conscious young adults.

Gratefully now navigating my life with this new spiritual foothold; I felt, once again, a deep yearning to be free from the anxiety that kept me playing small in life. Then one day I tried a particular modality that specifically addressed stress and trauma in the nervous system, and it stopped me in my tracks. I was euphoric; I knew I had found the missing piece of the puzzle.

This became another life altering time of transformation for me, as I rapidly started to experience profound and permanent changes in the fear that had kept me hiding from life. Remarkably, within a short period, I was speaking in front of a camera, performing on a stage with my band and doing interviews on the radio with ease! Fueled by the astonishing changes in my own ability to perform, my soul has been drawn to supporting people who are creative, artistic and in the spotlight. My passions continue both for deepening my knowledge of the spiritual and somatic worlds, and helping others bring their most powerful and brilliant expression of themselves out of hiding.

In the meantime, I still sing to the trees, dance every chance I get, and fiercely seek joy, play and exquisite sunsets.

What do I believe? That the truth you are seeking in life can be heard in the language of the spiritual and natural world around you, and will be communicated through your body's sensations. Become quiet, listen to the whisperings of these great wisdoms and welcome yourself into the realm of miracles, healing and grace.

IN PURSUIT OF THE DIVINE

Jennifer O'Neill

Jennifer O'Neill is a certified health and fitness coach who's on a mission to help other women spark their inner glow. She firmly believes that when we let our inner light shine, our outer world becomes a reflection of that light, and we can better serve and empower others on their journeys. Jennifer helps women live happier, healthier lives; full of joy and vibrancy!

🏠 www.luminouswellnesswithjennifer.com

📷 www.instagram.com/luminouswellnesswithjennifer

f www.facebook.com/luminouswellnesswithjennifer

CHAPTER 8

Spark Your Inner Glow

By Jennifer O'Neill

❧❧❧

Ever since I can remember, I've struggled with my weight. My mom says that I was thin when I was little and then all of a sudden gained all this weight in first grade. Although I wasn't often made fun of (surprisingly), I do distinctly remember being in Chile one summer, visiting my family, and two of my second cousins were laughing at me and calling me an elephant. The fact that I still remember that probably shows what a major impact it had on me, because to be honest, I don't remember a ton from my childhood.

Looking back, I think the sudden weight gain came about from the fact that I was stuffing down emotions from things that I saw happen between my mother and father. At that time, my father was an alcoholic, and although I don't remember any of it, I know that I witnessed him mistreating my mother. As a child, I didn't know how to process the emotions concerning the things that I was seeing.

I do remember that food started becoming a struggle. I was always hungry and wanting to eat something, and back then, my mother was living off her own income and supporting my brother, sister and I. We also had a nanny that took care of us, who was more like a grandmother. She showed her love for us via her cooking. I'm so thankful to have had her in my life, because together with my mother, she raised us.

As a result of using food to stuff down my emotions though, I've kept that trend going all the way through my adult life. I've been on every diet, have restricted, binged, worked out consistently, only to suddenly stop because I could see myself getting results. I had a fear of being different than what I was used to. I got to my highest weight of 220 pounds when I was in college because I was stressed and over eating. I cried many times over the rollercoaster, emotional turmoil that comes with constantly feeling like you're at odds with your body.

I've allowed myself to blame never having a boyfriend on my weight. I believed that no guy would ever love me because I wasn't thin, like society's portrayal of girls with boyfriends. I've used sex as a way to gain attention from guys, because getting some attention is better than nothing, *right*? I learned, though, that this was just another way to not treat my body with love. I was willing to offer myself to somebody who didn't truly care about me, and only wanted to use my body as a means to get pleasure for their own benefit. (Ironically, I've never been rejected by a guy sexually for being "too fat," so why did I think that a guy wouldn't love me because my body's not perfect?! It's ridiculous! A guy will love me for me!)

In my early 20s, I was diagnosed with PCOS, Polycystic Ovarian Syndrome, which is characterized by irregular periods, acne, hair growth in weird places, hair loss, infertility and difficulty losing weight, as a result of insulin resistance. I'm fortunate to say that I've managed to treat many of my PCOS symptoms holistically. After the medical system failed me time and time again, I took matters into my own hands and educated myself on ways to treat my body with care and love. Then later on in my 20s, I developed chronic pain, including a chronic daily headache that could often be debilitating. I believe all of these health issues developed partially as a result of keeping my emotions stuffed down. Being aware of that was the first step towards healing!

For a long time, I've wanted to hide, to not show my true self. I was afraid of speaking my truth and valuing what I had to offer. I still struggle with insecurities because even though I've managed to get to a healthier weight, I'm still not exactly where I want to be. As a result, I tell myself that it's still not enough. But what is enough anyway? What happens when you start loving your body as it is right now, despite what society or that voice inside your head tells you?

Through this process, I've deeply learned that the answer to anything that you want in life is never, EVER outside of yourself, as much as your ego might want you to think it is. The answer is always within, and the key is forgiveness. I don't blame my father or my mother or anyone else in my life for what has happened to me, or what appears to have happened to me. I have the power to change anything and everything deep within me. Learning to trust myself and just be the fullest expression of who I am has been a huge part of my journey.

I see what I've gone through up until this point in my life as a blessing, because it led me down a healthier lifestyle path and taught me how to care for myself, eat right, and start learning to treat my body with the love and respect it deserves. I've learned to keep going despite seeming obstacles, to be an example for people and show them that when you set your mind to something, absolutely anything is possible.

I'm done with "fighting" with myself because the truth is that my body is here to help me and protect me. I'm learning to treat it with love and everything that it deserves to have, because my body houses my soul and keeps me alive. It allows my heart to beat and gives me the opportunity to experience the beauty that all of this life has to offer.

As I mentioned earlier, I'm learning about the power of forgiveness. I've learned that when you throw anger or negative energy at something, it only expands whatever seems to be going wrong in your life. Meanwhile, forgiveness gives me the power to bestow love upon any situation. Forgiveness = *to give for*. It means to give for yourself and to give for another person through that process, and my goal is to make it a daily habit.

My own journey has been such a huge motivation for me to realize that my health issues partially developed as a result of not doing what I really want in life. Yes, I'm doing what society expects of me, which is having a steady job with an income and health insurance. Yet, that doesn't equate to what your soul wants on a higher level. And my soul spoke to me loud and clear when I decided to enroll in holistic health coaching school, and realized what I could do to help serve and empower other women as they navigate through their own journeys. I am so deeply grateful and thankful for everything that I've experienced. Without my seeming struggles, I wouldn't have discovered my life passion, which is helping and educating others via health and wellness. I'm leaving my job because it's no longer serving me at this point in my life.

Trust me, I'm not perfect. It's still a learning process for me. I still get annoyed sometimes that I eat really well and my body doesn't show much for it, and then I see other girls eating crap and their bodies stay thin. But at least I know that I'm healthy on the inside. And part of that comes with learning balance. Sometimes I want to eat junk (umm hello French fries or a gluten-free cupcake?!) and then allow myself to feel guilty for eating it. Really, why do we associate guilt with food? It's crazy! I'm learning that it's okay to eat foods that are not so okay sometimes, especially because my body reminds me how much better I feel when I eat really well! It's also a reminder to me that I have to learn to better trust and follow my intuition, work with my emotions whenever I get upset about something, and channel them through the power of forgiveness.

Spark Your Inner Glow came as a result of allowing that divine spark within me to shine forth as the fullest expression of myself. I already have everything that I could ever want or need already within me. I don't have to be the perfect weight, not that there is a perfect weight, or blindly follow what society teaches in order to achieve my own version of success. Yes, it's okay to take care of myself, to want to be my healthiest self, to love myself fully. It all stems from LOVE. Having struggled with binge eating for such a long time, I know that I've been seeking something outside of myself to feel fulfilled, which will never ever work. I cannot have a strong foundation for peace without love and forgiveness. Being the highest and truest version of myself creates miracles!

Peg Haust-Arliss,
LCSW-R, CCT, CACADP, NLP

Licensed psychotherapist, Life Strategist and Health Coach, Peg Haust-Arliss shares her story of fear to freedom as she recounts the birth of self-doubt, the path of a dream unfulfilled and the gift in disguise that forced her to reignite her spirit and take control of her life. Now living the dream she once believed impossible, Peg is the proud owner of Live More Coaching and Counseling, a thriving private practice in the beautiful Finger Lakes area of New York. Specializing in stress, anxiety and emotional fitness, Peg combines results oriented psychotherapy with holistic health coaching for effective and lasting change.

- 🏠 www.PegHaust.com
- 🏠 www.LiveMoreCoach.com
- f www.facebook.com/LifeCoachPeg
- 🐦 www.twitter.com/PegHaust

CHAPTER 9

From Fear to Freedom

By Peg Haust-Arliss, LCSW-R, CCT, AADP, NLP

క/6 ూ9

It's the night before my first day of school. I'm five years old, sitting on my dad's lap, full of hope and joy, asking him if I am going to learn to read tomorrow. "YES!" he said with an encouraging smile, "you will learn to read!" Dad didn't realize my literal inquiry: *Daddy, will I read fluently when I get home tomorrow?*

I couldn't contain my excitement, I was ready to GO! GO! GO!

From birth to five years old, I was pretty socially isolated, living in the county with lots of property, but not lots of kids. Before I entered the school system, I was surrounded by very loving parents, three older sisters and lots of fur friends. I felt loved and everyone treated me well. I was a happy-go-lucky little girl with a very bright spirit.

But, then came kindergarten...

My vision of that first day was nothing I had anticipated. Instead of learning to read, I learned I couldn't zip my zipper or tie my shoes fast enough. It looked to me that my classmates knew each other and had already established their groups. Although that was disappointing, it was nothing in comparison for what was to come: *Show n' Tell.*

Do you remember show n' tell? We were asked to bring something to school that we loved and show it to our classmates. One Christmas, I received the best gift ever; a battery operated dog that jumped and barked by remote control. I couldn't wait to share! The instructions were clear; form a seated circle on the floor, one at a time stand inside the circle, state your name, where you are from and present your beloved toys. Easy, cool, fun! *Right*? Well, not so much.

"HI! My name is Peggy Haust and I live in Tyre, NY"

At that moment roaring laughter surrounded me like a vortex from the floor. "HAHAHA!!! You live in a tire!!! HAHAHAHA!"

For me, this played out like the classic horror flick *Carrie*. Do you remember the famous scene after she was humiliated with the bucket of blood poured on her head? *They're laughing at you, they're all laughing at you!* Although likely not the case, that was my reality; they were all laughing *at* me! Not a great foundation for confidence. But kids are amazingly resilient; and by first grade, I was reignited because this is the year I *really was* going to read! Once again, I was out of my skin with excitement as we all sat on the floor facing the chalkboard to learn our first words.

"Does anyone know what this says?" My nice teacher asked.

My hand flew up like a rocket reaching for the stars. "PLEEEASE pick me!" Of course, she picked me. She must have thought I would pee my pants! "GO! GO! GO!" I exclaimed with a huge smile on my face.

"Yes, that's right Peggy." My teacher smiled back at me.

As I got a glimpse of my peers, however, they didn't seem as excited for me. To me, they had that "seriously...whatever?" look on their faces. I guess I needed to curb my enthusiasm.

I joke about it now, but what appeared to be meaningless events, were the birthplace of fears, phobias and insecurities that would imprison me for many years to come. I wanted to learn so badly, but what I was learning was to shrink down under the radar. Between that first "Carrie" episode in Kindergarten and its sequel in first grade, I learned to be quiet, to play small, and of course, to avoid public speaking at all costs.

Despite the early years of elementary school disillusionment, I never lost my appetite for growth and learning. Since age 17, I wanted to be a counselor. I knew, in the truthful place of my soul, that counseling was my strength and my calling. But, I had resigned myself to accept that this dream was not possible for me. Others, yes of course, but not for me. *I can't go to college, I'm not smart enough. Besides, how am I going to college with a severe public speaking phobia anyway?* So, I spent my twenties working various jobs in various fields trying to figure out a career that I could be at least content with.

But, dreams—this time of the nocturnal type—started to nag me. Periodically after high school and throughout my twenties, I had recurring dreams of walking down my high school hallways, crying because I missed it so much. I didn't give it much thought until age 29 when the dreams started to come on a regular basis. I could not ignore the message that was coming loud and clear as I approached my big 3-0 birthday: *It's time to make a decision, now or never.*

Turning 30, I chose NOW. I didn't know *how* I was going to get around the public speaking fears, but I had to figure it out. Being a talented and skilled avoider, I knew I would. *I won't tell anyone I'm going. That way, if I fail I can spare the embarrassment and humiliation.* Baby steps: *I'll start with a free continuing education course to see if I can even sit in a classroom without running out screaming. I will sit by the door just in case.*

During college, I was not *only* tested on paper. I was passionately learning and excelling academically beyond my wildest expectations, finally dispelling the "not smart enough" lie. But, the bigger I grew, so did the anxiety. The public speaking fear unexpectedly transformed into a debilitating panic disorder with agoraphobia— random feelings of irrational fear followed by the shame, disappointment and sadness of not having the ability to control it.

Life became very difficult and I lost the freedoms that most tend to take for granted. Daily tasks like driving, riding and errands were challenging. Things I had always enjoyed like traveling, going out dancing and shopping were out of the question. College was now a fearful event. I literally could not walk across the stage and accept my diplomas; my proudest moments turned to shame and sadness. Fear shrunk my world.

I tried therapy, but they suggested I see my doctor for a prescription. NOT what I was looking for. I wanted TOOLS, someone to tell me what to DO! But, I obliged since it appeared to be my only option. After a brief consult with an MD, I was given a script for Prozac. Of course, I didn't take it because medication was just another fear.

It is now 20 years later, and I am free from Anxiety State Prison! I finally did locate the tools for which I was looking. The first was cognitive therapy, where I learned to feed and condition my mind. Later, I understood the necessity of feeding my body and spirit. Through the years and lessons, I gathered a holistic toolbox; the same toolbox I now give to my clients.

The key to unlocking the cell door was within me the whole time! I NOW see that anxiety was, and still is, a gift. It's an evolutionary, instinctual gift given *for me* as an alert to danger or a reminder to prepare for life stages and responsibilities. And, it's also a personal gift because I truly believe I would not be in the position I am today, helping anxiety sufferers overcome their fears, if not for all I have experienced.

Anxiety is a necessary emotion, but it's not meant to be a prison sentence. I would have died in my soul, if I had not taken heed to those recurring dreams warning me to GET OUT! Now there's a *real* horror flick! Do I still experience anxiety? Absolutely! In fact, a while ago while driving to the airport, old familiar feelings of panic returned in full force. What was going on!? I hadn't experienced driving anxiety in years! I was freaking out on the thruway and called a friend for support.

I realized the anxiety was occurring because I needed to decide on a new and unknown course, a path that would, once again, push me into new growth and opportunities. It had been quite some time since I stretched so far outside my comfort zone. Anxiety was showing up, as it did years ago, to keep me safe and sound; to make sure I kept my shine meter in check. But, there was no danger, nothing from which to keep me safe. It was just a growth spurt with some added growing pains. Now, the question was, do I decide to dim my light, play small or live with freedom? By getting on the plane, I realized I had already decided. I smiled to myself: *GO, GO, GO GIRL, it's time to show n' tell!*

"Shining star for you to see what your life can truly be"

Earth, Wind and Fire, 1975

IN PURSUIT OF THE DIVINE

Kathy Dailey

Kathy Dailey is a professional coach and creative consultant whose expertise helps individuals and organizations get "unstuck" from their personal and professional roadblocks. Her authentic style and sense of humor helps guide clients through their journey of self-discovery and self-expression. Kathy provides the tools needed to help her clients understand the power of recognizing and using their innate spiritual wisdom.

Dailey is a New Ventures West Certified Integral Coach PCC.

📞 **(323) 791-5211**

✉ **kadailey@pacbell.net**

CHAPTER 10

Finding My Way Home

By Kathy Dailey

ᘔᘔᘔ

"Oh my God. I'm in such pain I can hardly breathe. I feel like every cell in my body is on fire, and at the same time, every cell in my body is crying. I'm lying on the floor in a fetal position sobbing and moaning, with my heart so raw it feels like it's bleeding. By body, my life, my soul is being torn apart, and I'm in a free-fall. I find myself screaming, "What is going on?!"

What was this gut wrenching experience? And why did it happen to me?

Let's go back to my late 20s when I arrived in Los Angeles. I had grown up in a northern Michigan town with one main street, one cinema and no fast food. I enjoyed ice fishing with my father, hanging out at the diner and putting colored lights on deer antlers for the holidays. I was living in East Lansing after college when my ex-boyfriend called on a freezing day and volunteered to drive us to sunny Los Angeles. It was an offer I couldn't resist. So, we packed up my station wagon and drove across country. When we first crested the highway that looks out over the San Fernando Valley, I experienced a panoramic view of lights that glittered in the distance. Here was my Oz; but unlike Dorothy, I didn't own a pair of magical ruby slippers.

I settled in the depths of the San Fernando Valley, an arid area of tract homes and strip malls. I hadn't expected Munchkins waving lollipops, but I also didn't expect to dislike it as much as I did. There was too much sunshine, too many freeways and too many people obsessed with making money.

Like most college graduates, I didn't know how to do anything. I could barely type and I was extremely shy. But little by little, I landed odd jobs in the entertainment industry as a receptionist or an accounting assistant. I got fired quite a few times along the way because I didn't have the required skills. I was starting to feel desperate when a college friend asked if I wanted to work in the box office at the Pantages Theatre in Hollywood. I was dedicated, passionate and a quick study and worked my way up the ladder. I became my friend's executive assistant, and eventually was asked to manage the in-house advertising agency where I learned the art of copywriting, as well as television, radio and print production.

By this time I was in my mid-30s and enjoying a fast-paced life dictated by the demands of Hollywood; lots of sex, drugs and rock n' roll. Cue the flying monkeys! I was still talking my way into jobs, but I was much more adept at staying on the job until I figured it out. Through good fortune and the kindness of people who gave me an opportunity, I ended up working at two major television stations, and a number of advertising and media companies. I met an incredibly loving man, and had the good sense to marry him. (This after dating and almost marrying men who were also good – just not good for me!) Life was pretty damn good.

My fast-paced life soon got a wake-up call when my best friend and potential business partner was diagnosed with a brain tumor at the age of 43. I watched her waste away into nothingness. She died slowly; she died quickly. And her death dimmed all the sparkling lights that had seemed so important to me. I dropped out of the industry and just drifted along, too numb and too angry to want to do much of anything. And like Dorothy, I spent days "asleep" in my own private poppy field. I eventually worked as a creative consultant and media coach, but realized I no longer had a passion for the work. I felt stuck. I felt depressed. I felt lost.

I was in the perfect place to hear a colleague suggest I consider becoming a coach. I did my research and applied to a school in San Francisco. It had a sterling reputation and a rigorous curriculum. I filled out the papers and waited to hear when I would start this new adventure. But when I got a letter saying I was rejected, I was dumfounded. Luckily, there was an opportunity to reapply. I sent another application and was declined a second time. This rejection put me in a tailspin. I was going to pay them a substantial amount of money and they didn't want me! I was in shock and terribly hurt. But also, I realized that this path was something I really wanted.

I swallowed my pride and called to see if there was anything else I could do to gain admittance. I talked to a faculty member and discovered that they were concerned about my lack of spirituality and my need to be constantly stimulated. Their impression was that I wasn't suited for this type of work. This was just the first in a series of challenges I faced during that year of study. It was grueling and it constantly knocked me off balance. It was a process that eventually made me feel so raw, it was like I had the skin ripped off my body. It made me question everything I had ever thought and experienced.

There were many times during this yearlong immersion that I wanted to stop the process of dismantling the formulated beliefs, concepts and stories that had made me feel safe. I was skeptical of the books and teachings that encouraged me to live with uncertainty and not be overly concerned with how to make sense of everything. I found myself in a constant state of anxiety, and saw the sparkling lights of my Emerald City fading in the distance. It made me realize I had an emptiness inside that could only be filled by a spiritual practice.

During the last six months of the program, I experienced a feeling of profound sadness. I often felt like I was slogging through mud both physically and emotionally. On other days, I felt like my hair was on fire and my body was vibrating so violently I might spin off the planet. And then there was the day I had a complete breakdown. The day I described at the beginning of this chapter, when I was sobbing on the floor in a fetal position. The day I was calling out to God to help me understand what was going on!! The crying went on for hours, and when I couldn't cry anymore, I felt a profound sense of peace come over me. I realized that I had finally let go. I didn't know where I was going or what I was becoming, but I was at peace with being in the unknown.

I continued my quest to find a spiritual home that led to a Buddhist meditation center. The teachings and practices felt foreign yet familiar and no one ever asked me what I did for a living. And after a year of shedding my skin and growing a new one, I obtained a coaching certificate and felt validated in a way that transcended anything I had achieved previously.

During my journey down the yellow brick road, like the Scarecrow, I had developed my brain; and like the Cowardly Lion, overcoming fear had encouraged me to be brave. But unlike the Tin Man, I already had a heart. Although little did I know that my heart wasn't awake. My heart didn't have an understanding of how the act of self-cherishing causes pain, and love grows when you soften your heart. This awareness went against the "me, me, me" of Hollywood, which tends to create a lot of magic tricks to keep the Wizard in power.

I now had my own magic. Magic based on spiritual teachings that enabled me to relax and be comfortable with always being uncomfortable; to remember to check my ego at the door when working with clients, because it wasn't about me, it was never about me. It's about opening my heart and mind to the spiritual wisdom that's inside each of us. It's about gaining a deeper understanding of unconditional love and support. It's about coaxing my heart and mind to expand to the outer edges of my universe, knowing that this experience will come full circle when I coach.

As a certified Integral Coach, I have enjoyed encouraging clients to explore their own yellow brick roads. As a fellow traveler, I know that our brains, courage and heart will be tested. But unlike Dorothy, we don't have to click our heels to get home. We know we always have a home. Our home is beating within us. And it will travel with us when we leave this beautiful planet. Our home is forever.

IN PURSUIT OF THE DIVINE

Charmayne Olswang, CHHC, ACADP

Charmayne Olswang has been a coach and mentor from an early age. Although for many years she followed society's standards and benchmarks for success, she was guided back to her heart's song and God-given purpose. She is certified in Holistic Health and Transformational Life Coaching, as well as, ways to connect to one's higher calling. She works with clients who want to make changes in their daily lives in order to reach their health and lifestyle goals. These desires may include obtaining more energy, managing weight, stress, and anxiety and making better choices for themselves and their families.

🏠 FeelLoveHeal.com

f www.facebook.com/FeelLoveHeal

🐦 www.twitter.com/FeelLoveHeal

CHAPTER 11

Feel. Love. Heal.

By Charmayne Olswang, CHHC, AADP

❧✦❧

Reflecting as far back into my memory as possible, in search of what guided me to where I am today, millions of flashes from my past cross my mind like film on a movie screen. There is no music, just images. At first they skim the surface, frivolous and Pollyanna-like, perhaps how I "wished" my history had taken place. As I sit quietly in observation and contemplation, I keep getting the same scene. It is a repetitively different scenario, yet holds the identical core feelings permanently bruised on my heart. Distrust. Sad. Unsafe. Alone. All stemming from alcohol related memories.

I hesitate and hastily search for different recollections. Others superficially appear, but I am deeply reminded of the indisputable. I desperately aspire that my memory be something more comfortable to share in this forum, to no avail. Each retrospection and disagreeable feeling boomerangs to a crystal clear picture of a little girl, independent beyond her years, strong, athletic, confident, funny, outgoing, smart, beautiful, confused, sad, worried, anxious, isolated, searching... emotionally maturing much faster than her peers.

I grew up in a divorced family, an only child to my parents whom separated when I was a baby. I did not have a formal religious foundation. I believed in God and Jesus. I trusted there was a Heaven and most likely Hell. I knew the sign of the cross, and sometimes said prayers quietly to myself while falling asleep. I was never aware of there being a Higher Power taking care of me or having my life pre-determined. I did not know the depth of spirituality or any way in which to connect to it.

For as far back as my emotional connection allows me, my life was largely consumed by days at the beach, having fun with my mom, her friends and their children and weekend parties with a profusion of alcohol. The music was loud and the laughter abundant, while the adults enjoyed each other's company and all of us stayed up WAY past a decent bedtime.

My young mom, our medley of roommates and their friends knew how to have fun. Even though I was often times included and knew, *without a doubt,* that so many people loved me, I learned early on that I could not, and did not, trust a drunk. I did not feel safe or protected around them. I innately knew that my best interest was NOT a top priority when an alcoholic had authority. Their words were not reliable. Their lips were often filled with exaggerated stories of whatever sounded good in the moment.

Ironically, or not as the case may be, I would eventually search for and find exactly *that* in the man I would marry. Regardless of my past, I choose and love my husband with all my heart, just as I do my mom, stepdad and all the "grown-ups" that helped raise me along the way. This is not to shame, embarrass or blame ANY of them; it simply *is* what is; my story of growing up Charmayne.

As much as I honor the experiences of my childhood, after all they have developed me into the unstoppable woman I am today; at that time, I was often envious of the kids at school being dropped off and kissed goodbye by their parent while I independently walked or rode myself to school. At lunchtime, I would watch with anticipation as they opened their sack lunch and I would intriguingly look for their note of endearment written either on the bag or napkin, while I insecurely took out my self-made "sandwich", consisting of Roman Meal bread and French's mustard. I did love mustard and was proud of myself for making it, which was more than they could say of their multi-layered, multi-colored, restaurant style delicacy. But, I also longingly wished I had their seemingly beautiful, "perfect" life.

Despite what I assumed was going on in the families around me; I embraced my independence and prided myself on being someone the other kids ran to, to "protect" them. I have always felt an intrinsic need to take care of others and myself.

The beginning of my deeper relationship with God and Spirituality developed in 2008, when I made the decision to attend an Al Anon 12-Step Program. I was shocked to find a support system that had so much knowledge and wisdom in the cunning disease of alcoholism. I watched in disbelief while these people laughed and smiled as though life was happy and joyful, all while sharing stories of their experience, strength and hope, with the rest of us. I began to learn that my life was not mine to forcefully control; rather, I was here to live God's purpose for me, knowing He had my back and the people, events and circumstances I endured were all part of this Divine process. God was preparing me, training me and testing me.

Gratefully, my pursuit of the Divine was a vacuum of curiosity and calling, which has markedly helped me resolve unexplained characteristics and behaviors that were disseminated into my little mind from a very young age. This newfound awareness unmasked what God had programmed into my soul—the feeling of never wanting to rely on others to do things for me, and serving as caretaker for those in need.

Whether this was nurture or nature and probably a bit of both, I did not count on many people. Contrarily, many people depended on me. When I did lean on someone else, I felt extremely unstable, insecure, unsure, enslaved and obligated, all disempowering and weak feelings. I protected myself by not counting on others.

The tide began to shift. History gets to be rewritten, as the child becomes the mother:

Due to the fact that I have never felt safe around heavy drinkers, I have made it a priority to do for my children what the adults in my life did not do for me. I work diligently to make them feel safe and KNOW that they can trust and depend on me, always, at all times and in all circumstances. I am determined that the childhood I experienced will not be a reality my children will endure.

Even though I married into an alcoholic family, I chose an amazing man to raise and nurture our children. He is everything I am not, and takes care of them in ways I have never before seen a man contribute. He is perfect. He has a disease. I adore him anyway, just as one would a loved one with cancer or diabetes. And **that** is perfect.

With an endless amount of appreciation for God and the path he placed before me in my upbringing, I consciously and continually choose to make my children feel confident knowing that they can rely on me, just as I do Spirit. In my ever-evolving Divine pursuit, I regularly check in with God, ask for His guidance and trust in His plan. I have faith that He is protecting me and looking over me at all times. I am restored. I am safe.

Today, I live my life from a place of immense gratitude and dedication. I value and appreciate my experiences. Positive and negative, each and every one of them has had an impact on developing the amazing woman I am today. I am an incredible human being, and I do not need anyone else to tell me this. Of course it feels comforting and extraordinary when they do, but I no longer NEED that. I know, in the deepest depth of my heart and soul that I am perfect, just as I am, and am not. In times of quandary, I choose to lean on the Serenity Prayer:

God, grant me the serenity to accept the things I cannot change, the courage to change the things I can, and the wisdom to know the difference.

It is very clear to me that I have answered my absolute assignment, given to me by the Creator. I am here to guide others (especially women) to love and enjoy themselves for who they are and what they have overcome in their past. I am inspired to support, teach, coach and speak to those in our world that continue to hold themselves hostage to a yesterday they cannot change. Their history may be just days ago, or perhaps what feels like another lifetime ago. No matter the time period, for every second that we stay paralyzed by what we cannot control, we lose precious moments of our Divine gift…the Present.

If no one has told you today, I am here to tell you: You are Beautiful! You are MORE than enough! You deserve to live and enjoy the life your inner child has always dreamed! And…I Love You!

IN PURSUIT OF THE DIVINE

Maggie Chula

Maggie Chula, Spiritual Healer and Direct Channel for the Archangels and Ascended Masters, shares her message of healing through the use of sacred wisdom. She shares the process that she endured, which proves the importance of healing as a daily lifestyle choice.

Maggie is the creator and teacher of *Open the Doorway to Your Soul: The Akashic Vibration Process*, a leadership development and training program for spiritual healing. Maggie's passion is to help people connect to the Light of their Soul, and learn how to access their sacred wisdom to transform their health, life and world.

🏠 www.MaggieChula.com

f www.facebook.com/MaggieChulaToo

𝕏 www.twitter.com/maggie_chula

in www.linkedin.com/in/maggiechula

CHAPTER 12

Sacred Wisdom

By Maggie Chula

ℰ⁄ᛜᛜℒ

I was born with a weak immune system, feet turned inward that required leg braces and steel shoes to correct, and a very strong and personal knowledge of the spiritual realm. During the many illnesses and events of my early childhood, I was always aware of my guides and angels. It was very comforting in their energetic field when I sensed them around me.

I became even more aware of them when I had my first near death experience. I was four years old. I was caught in our dining room when the bathroom came crashing down as the top floor gave way. I was knocked unconscious and stopped breathing. I remember being surrounded by a feeling of loving compassion and warmth. I was instructed to go back and I woke up on the living room couch with my mother crying over me. After my connection to the wonderful vibration of the Source and the angels, I was able to heal my body one issue at a time.

There were many Divine beings who were always around. They taught me how to work with my mind so I could live within my body and stay connected to them.

Health issues continued to be a problem. These issues were so apparent, my siblings and I joked that I was born on the wrong planet. I was allergic to basic foods, including pepper. Once when I was five, my throat became so swollen after eating something with pepper, I actually thought I would die from suffocation. I was diagnosed with many allergies including the air during any type of weather but spring and fall were the worst; indoor allergens from pets, both dogs and cats; dust, trees, and the list was endless and overwhelming. It was my allergy to trees, however, that allowed me to understand the power that beliefs have in healing the body.

By the time I agreed to allergy testing, I was congested most of the time and had daily bouts of headaches. I had two young children, a husband, two cats and a full time job as a Project Leader in Information Systems for a large, international corporation. I was overwhelmed and out of energy.

During the testing, the nurse injected my arm with various substances. I showed mild to average allergic reactions to everything she tested. I was growing very uneasy about the process. Finally, there was a very large and immediate response to her injections. She was excited, I was curious and relieved we could stop. She circled the area and told me the severe reaction would help them create a serum to ease my headaches.

I looked at the large bump on my arm and asked, "What is it?" She told me it was pine trees. Without thinking, I stated very clearly that I was not allergic to trees. The reaction immediately left my arm. She was bewildered and asked what I had just done. The reaction on my arm was gone. If the circle had not been there we would not have had any evidence that I had shown any reaction at all.

I thought about it; and I realized, I loved trees. I loved their life force, their colors; the way birds used them for homes. I loved everything about trees. I knew in my heart I was not allergic to trees. With that very intense and determined mindset, the reaction within my body changed immediately. This was a defining moment for me. For at that moment, I realized how much I had been healing myself on certain levels, but I needed more information to heal other areas of my body I knew were weak. That was the start of a very long and intense road to studying the process of self-healing.

I had done healing work on myself and others. Those healings, however, were done with the help of my guides and on a fairly unconscious level. By the time I found myself in the doctor's office getting allergy tests, my life was overwhelmingly stressful. That is when I found myself without enough energy, time or motivation to truly heal myself to the level my body needed.

I felt, at that point in my life, I needed to stop my natural healing methods and allow the medical doctors to help me figure out what was wrong with my body. I wanted them to find out what was wrong so I could get some medicine and move on with my life. It took a while to figure out the root cause of the weakness within my body. By the time they had a final diagnosis, I had ulcers in my mouth, going down my throat and all the way through my intestinal tract. After the reaction to my thoughts at the allergist's office many months before, I had stopped trying to fix things. What I didn't realize was how long it would take the doctors to find what was wrong and how sick I would become.

The doctors tried every test to find the root cause of my health issues. I became very weak. I felt like a zombie. I couldn't think anymore. Yet, I believed I was going to be able to heal. I just needed to know what was wrong.

On the day I was scheduled for a test at the hospital, I woke up with huge black and blue welts all over my body. I looked like I had been beaten with a baseball bat. My husband had to carry me into the hospital because I was too weak to walk. The testing that day confirmed I had an acute case of Crohn's Disease.

My doctor was very serious when he shared the diagnosis with me. He explained I needed to have surgery as soon as possible; but in my weakened state, I would not survive. I was too weak for surgery. He felt it would take four weeks before I would be well enough. I asked that he explain what a diagnosis of Crohn's Disease meant. *How was my intestinal tract damaged and different from a healthy one?* He pointed out where my body was grey in tissue and should have been pink. It was at that moment, I realized I hadn't been watching a black and white monitor. My internal organs were grey and very sick.

I used the time—those four weeks given to me—to get well enough for surgery, and change my daily routine. With the help of the Angels, I created a guided visualization audio to help me heal my whole body. I listened to that guided visualization at least twice a day. I drank water and gave up pop and coffee. Within a week, I was doing slightly better. Within two weeks, I was able to add a few exercises to help my body get stronger. At the end of four weeks, I was feeling much better.

On my way to getting my strength back, my doctor wanted to schedule the surgery. I felt so good, I didn't want to. I believed I would continue to heal through the use of my new daily routine and I did.

As my body responded to my process and I grew in the knowledge of how to keep my life and my body in harmony, I have learned to tweak my daily routine to support the changes that took place in my life. New exercises get added. The guided visualizations change. I had learned, in order to keep and sustain the healing within my physical body, I needed to keep a balance in all areas of my life. I needed a daily connection to the light of my soul and the loving vibration I felt. I needed to work on my health and my soul connection each day.

The lowest point in my body's health came when my children were two and four, and I was unable to take care of my own basic needs. I had to have someone bath me, feed me and take care of my children. I had trouble getting out of bed by myself.

My children are adults now. I am very healthy. I have never had surgery for Crohn's Disease, or for any other medical reason. I have had a few flare ups within the past two decades; and I admit, medicine helps me when I need to take it, but I do not take any medication on a daily basis. I have learned to listen to my body and my divine angelic council. Through that connection, I am able to attain and maintain a wonderful balance of health in all areas of my life.

I am blessed to work in the spiritual healing field. Each day, I consciously work to connect my clients and students to their higher wisdom so they are able to create a healthy balanced life in alignment with their soul's purpose.

IN PURSUIT OF THE DIVINE

Christel Arcucci

Christel Arcucci is the founder Mindful Living Arts and creator of Soul Centered Prosperity. She is an International Healer, Artist, Transformational Speaker, Prosperity Coach, & Trainer. She is known as the healer's healer. Christel is a catalyst for healers, holistic practitioners, and coaches to alchemize their "struggling healer" story into prosperity, play & a pleasurable business & life. She is passionate about empowering women to be seen, heard & financially supported through their soul purpose. Christel has supported thousands of clients to integrate being spiritual, sexy, and successful with her holistic lifestyle & prosperity system since 1991.

🏠 www.ChristelArcucci.com

f www.facebook.com/ChristelArcucci1

▶ www.youtube.com/user/christelarcucci

🐦 www.twitter.com/christelarcucci

CHAPTER 13

Woman and Healer Transformed by Fire

By Christel Arcucci

As a young girl, I developed a powerful connection to an inner imaginary world. I was raised in a conservative and wealthy suburb of Chicago that I did not understand nor connect to. I was a sensitive child in an unstable and dysfunctional household. I would retreat to the realm of spirit and the outdoors which gave me solace yet left me feeling alone and confused trying to understand my intuition and visions which I would later discover were past life scenes. I longed for freedom and to openly share the depth of the real me. I wanted to speak the truth and to creatively express my deep soul knowing. It was painful to know I had to wait until I was an adult.

♦ ♦ ♦

It was a school morning at the breakfast table with the autumn sun streaming in the kitchen window. My mother had remarried in the summertime and my 7 year old sister was struggling to swallow a vitamin when my step father said, "your boyfriends will appreciate it if you learn to swallow." My jaw dropped and I glared at mother in the awkward silence that followed this outrageous remark. She averted her eyes and said, "come on Laura, just swallow it." I was 12 years old, I was afraid, angry and felt an intense fire inside as my mother was unknowingly demonstrating that she was unable to protect us against her new husband.

This moment was the beginning of the end of my relationship with my mother; deep inside, I knew I should prepare for her to betray me. Within a year, I would move into my father's home due to my step-fathers inappropriate behavior which my mother refused to acknowledge and seemed helpless to change. When I left her home, she said, "don't come back, you are no longer my daughter." My heart broke with the flash of fire inside that felt as if I was being burned alive. It would be 5 years before I would know that is "burning" sensation was related to visions of past lives when I had been burned at the stake for being a woman with power, a healer, and a witch.

Twenty-eight years later, I stand with quiet strength in a room full of heart-centered women entrepreneurs. We have gathered for a two-day transformational business mastermind. I am at the front of the room in the "hot seat," while my colleagues sit comfortably on couches in an elegant, homey setting.

"What will happen if you are visible? What will happen if the world sees your full power? Don't think — just answer," my mentor commands.

"I will be killed."

I stand between worlds with one foot in present time and the other in a past life. A woman in the room gasps and tears stream down my cheeks. I speak of being burned at the stake as empowered woman and healer.

"I am no longer afraid of being killed because I know that my essence, my soul cannot be destroyed. They tortured and killed the tribe of women healers that I led. They made me watch as each one of my soul sisters died a terrible death. I begged for them to spare my sisters and just kill me. I died with every woman before they destroyed my body. I made a vow that I would never again put the lives of my sisters in jeopardy. I committed to traveling alone: When they find and kill me the next time, no one else will die because of me."

My heart breaks open as the scene unfolds in vivid detail. Both my present reality and my past life as revolutionary leader are so tangible, and powerfully connected. I don't have proof that I have lived other lives, yet this vision forces me to resolve this past-life saga in this very lucid moment of now.

I want to crumble, to give up and disappear. My shadow, that part of me I have been unwilling — unable — to embrace, is demanding that I recognize its power. I have spent years hiding and suppressing the magnitude of the fear, power, and rage inside me. I am keenly aware of the great potential that lies in alchemizing these base emotions. I see my self-imposed shackles with crystal clarity.

◆ ◆ ◆

For the past 24 years, I have been a professional healer and artist. But until that auspicious day in 2013, I had been playing small and staying safe, allowing fear of persecution to stop me. I justified my circumstances and convinced myself that the level of service I was providing in my healing arts business was enough – that I could fulfill my soul purpose without stepping too far outside my comfort zone.

A few years ago, I was called to awaken greater potential as not only a healer but as a revolutionary leader of healers. I resisted that inner voice, because I did not feel ready to step into this role of empowering women. I would tell myself that someday I would be ready, someday ...

In late 2008, I made the commitment to get the mentoring and business training necessary to take my business to the next level. Out of that commitment came a series of synchronicities that eventually brought me to that gathering, where, steeped in a cauldron of sisterly support, the story continues ...

◆ ◆ ◆

I am being confronted by my mentor in present time, and I can feel the strength of the invisible field that keeps me from stepping into the leadership role I know I was born to fill. Although I want to support women to claim their power as fully activated healers, that outdated promise keeps me stagnant.

She stands before me, extending a deeply compassionate yet unwavering invitation: *"The women from that life are looking for you lead them now. Will you show up for them?"*

I feel the strength of her call, beckoning me to unleash the potency of my mission, to serve as a beacon of light that others will follow.

In a flash I see that my persistent refusal to show up in my full splendor (cloaked as valiant loyalty to a sacred vow) is the most destructive and selfish choice I could make. My resistance to lead dissolves in an instant.

The old victim story of fear and persecution literally vanishes as I stand in my power: *"Yes, I will show up for them."*

The victim story is only part of the truth. In other lives I have perpetrated the hunting and killing. An unacknowledged aspect of my soul is capable of murder, destruction, and torture. I know in every moment we are free to choose to create or destroy life. In order to break the cycle of victim > rescuer > perpetrator, I must face the aspects inside me that are capable of such darkness.

The room dissolves and my mentor and I are dressed in priestess robes in a forest clearing where the past is completed and the present moment merges with a future time.

She says, *"now is the first time in thousands of years that you are safe to reclaim your place of power. It is time to take on your sacred role as a leader in the sisterhood. You are protected and guided. Will you reclaim your place of power?"*

"Yes, I will. Thank you."

My mentor reminds me of my mother, this potent moment of her inviting me into my power heals my mother's betrayal while activating a mystical path into my future. I know in my bones that my ability to create and destroy will be used in service of life and love. In the moment I claimed my power and released the old beliefs, I ended the victim cycle that had undermined my power as a woman and leader. I integrate the light and the dark to embrace all of me and activate my full power.

◆ ◆ ◆

My life purpose of guiding women to reach their highest potential is unfolding with ease. I empower heart-centered women entrepreneurs to activate their healing gifts and make money while making a positive difference. Together we create magic, beauty, financial abundance, and healing for ourselves and our communities. We are activating soul centered prosperity in life, love, and business, while reestablishing the sisterhood in present time.

It is safe to openly share our healing gifts ... *Will you join me?*

The sisterhood welcomes you to take your place in the circle.

Delight in the divine union of masculine and feminine,
the light and the dark forces within.

Activate your power for healing.
Embrace the darkness of your shadow.

Claim the fierce power of the fire, to create and destroy.

Listen to the whispering of your soul, calling you home ...
to yourself, your truth, your power, and your healing.

As you heal yourself, you will heal your family and community.

Allita C. Parlette, AADP

Having found her way to a beautiful metamorphosis after cancer, menopause and alcoholism, Allita Parlette is fulfilling her life's purpose by providing the love and guidance for others to find their own transformation.

As a Certified Health Coach and vivacious thriver, Allita knows that life is far from over after 50. She started her company, Ellaquent Consulting, LLC to combine holistic nutritional coaching with what she calls wardrobe therapy. Allita is passionate about coaching women on how to find their truest selves, improve their inner balance and reflect that with an outer expression that is empowering, confident and self accepting.

✉ aparlette@ellaquent.net

🏠 www.ellaquent.net

🅱 www.restartbuttonap.blogspot.com

f www.facebook.com/allita.parlette

CHAPTER 14

Beautiful Metamorphosis

By Allita C. Parlette, AADP

༺ ༻

In April 2011 at the age of 48 I was diagnosed with colon cancer. While not life-ending, this would prove to be life-changing and profoundly transformational. At that time, having so sense of purpose, I was living a life that was completely out of alignment with who I am … alcoholic drinking, demoralizing sexual behavior, extravagant spending and frenetic traveling. I had become like a wildly spinning top, never actually touching the earth or slowing down long enough to see things for what they were. The dis-ease in my body, and what came afterwards, proved to be a long overdue call to heal my wounded spirit and finally live an authentic life.

Beautiful Metamorphosis because the butterfly has become my symbol of transformation. You see butterflies were my mother's thing, and I never took much notice of them until one day, after she had passed, when I did. She was sending me her usual brand of loving message: My caterpillar life would soon be over, and it might feel like a death. I would need to cocoon for a while, to heal and rebuild; to go from what was, to what was always meant to be. And one day when the time was right, I would step from that sheltering cocoon into a beautiful new life, spread my wings and bravely leave the old life behind me.

To begin with, despite my parents' best efforts to instill in me a sense of self and individuality, what always mattered most to me was the acceptance of others, never my own. After the devastating loss of my father when I was 14, and being sexually assaulted when I was

17, drinking soon became how I felt acceptable to others and, in fact, to myself. In short, drinking enabled me to be "more" … more comfortable with myself, with intimate relationships and with the world as a whole. But over the years, as I focused only on trying to be what I thought others wanted me to be, the relationship with myself withered from lack of attention.

The gift that cancer ended up being for me is how it forced me to slow down, to look at myself and see what that withered self image was doing to my health and my life. I was in the hospital for a month recovering from surgeries, then almost immediately started on chemotherapy for several months. I had nothing but time, time where I was not physically able to do much of anything and had to learn to just be. And in that quiet space the top finally stopped spinning and I began to realize that the life I was living was not the life I wanted. Cancer also showed me that I wasn't immortal, that my life was finite and if I wanted a different reality for myself, now was the time to make that happen.

Spiritually I had always believed in a higher power, but I was not raised in an environment where the word God was familiar at all, let alone the concept of prayer. One night, towards the end of my hospital stay, feeling completely drained of every single spiritual reserve that had carried me that far and all out of options, I finally turned to God and asked for help. Afterwards, I can only describe what I felt as "being held"; it was an extremely powerful moment in my life. I went from a very empty, lonely feeling of free-falling with no net to knowing that I was not alone, that I was standing on solid ground and someone had my back. In one moment my life changed forever and I am grateful every day that it did.

That experience taught me, among many other things, that to achieve my greatest healing I needed to tune into my own intuition, which I now believe is God communicating with me. I did this first by telling my doctors what I would and would not accept as treatment plans, including stopping my chemotherapy early. My entire being was telling me that was the right thing to do. I knew it was right because when I was resolved I felt confident, fearless and empowered. When fear was let in for a short time, I felt weak, I cried constantly and that feeling of empowerment was gone - I was miserable. But my inner wisdom, my faith, spoke louder inside of me. I once again became resolved, the tears stopped and I felt strong in my decision. Since then, every single thing that has happened has reaffirmed for me that my intuition was right, and I thank God that I was open to trusting that inner wisdom.

That intuition also led me to enroll in a health coaching program to heal myself, with a sense that destiny was calling to me. In that program, I learned two very powerful lessons that resonated deeply and led to much healing: Our bodies know what they need and will tell us if we listen, and that every one of us is different. For the first time in my life, I began to tune out what "they" said was good or bad nutritionally and instead listened to what my own body was trying to tell me.

When I listen to what is inside of me, I don't just survive, I thrive. Someone suggested some body image work to focus on expressing not love for, but just acceptance of, the areas of my body that had changed so much. That overall message of acceptance is so gentle, and now that I have seen what happens when I turn from that, it has a resounding impact on my entire being. As I became willing to forgive, accept and even love my body, I was able to release over 30 pounds of inflammation and weight, along with debilitating pain.

By listening to my own inner voices again, I eventually realized that I could not continue ignoring that elephant in the room — my drinking. Louise Hay says that cancer is the result of a deep hurt, a longstanding resentment eating away at the self. I drank to avoid feeling the pain that I had held onto, and that pain was like a malignancy eating away at me ... that malignancy became my cancer. Tuning into myself to heal physically helped me to finally see that the time had come to cut away that old dead scar tissue and begin to truly heal.

My healing journey eventually brought me to the rooms of a recovery program for alcoholism in January 2013. The road to recovery is full of uncomfortable moments and unfamiliar territory. But faith in this process enables me to just "be" with my discomfort, to walk through it instead of numbing through it. Once I surrendered fully I knew there was no turning back for me. I stay mindful of how far I have come and that there is something much bigger and more lovingly powerful than me in control of all of this. My heart and soul are so much calmer and more peaceful now that I have stopped running from the darkness and pain. My inner child is healing, she is learning to trust me again and I am so very grateful for this second chance with her.

I was able to create a cocoon for myself out of quiet spaces, self-acceptance, physical and emotional healing, faith in something greater than myself, and surrender. I surrounded myself with only that which nurtured, supported, encouraged and empathized. The only voices that existed in my cocoon were those I allowed in, and I refused to allow my own voice to speak against me. For me, it was not about putting myself first on the list, it was and still is about putting myself ON the list in the first place.

This transformational process also included turning 50 and experiencing surgical menopause — two rights of passage that were, for me, very traumatic and eventually very empowering. I feel like a member of The Club now ... women who have made it past 50, survived and thrived through life-changing events like menopause, illness and heartache. It is a club that I am extremely proud to be a member of.

Today, having emerged from my nurturing cocoon, I know that I am right where I am meant to be. I understand that all of my pain, heartaches, joys, breakdowns and breakthroughs were gifts given to me so my reason for being here, for being who I am, could crystalize. I had to experience these events in order to know my value and my purpose. I now have the tools to help others and to pay it forward. In a beautiful metamorphosis, I am transformed into a being whose purpose is love, love is why I am here. From now on, I will also be including myself in that love.

"Be yourself, everyone else is already taken."
– Oscar Wilde

Melissa Erin Monahan,
M.A., LCAT

Melissa Erin Monahan, M.A., LCAT is a passionate and co-creative facilitator of transformation on the deepest level of identity. A Certified Conscious Uncoupling, Calling in "The One" and Feminine Power transformative coach, as well as licensed creative arts therapist, Melissa offers group workshops in the New York City-Metro Area and private coaching worldwide.

"Melissa is a master who has a gift for healing, helping and transcending. I have been a consumer of all things therapy, self-help and 12-steps for 20 years. I can honestly say this was the most successful experience." ~ Michelle, New York City

Visit melissaerinmonahan.com or femininecocreator.com

CHAPTER 15

Becoming a Feminine Co-Creator

By Melissa Erin Monahan, M.A., LCAT

❧

The year: 1978

The scene: My grandparents' living room

It's Easter Sunday and *The Wizard of Oz* is playing on the huge television set. Age 2, I am mesmerized by Judy Garland's every move as Dorothy. Something significant is happening within my being. It feels like an identity reunion. Pure potential explodes in my every cell. I never want the sensation to stop because *this is me.* Even for my young consciousness, the encounter feels magical, deeply relational, loving and, well, *holy.* Recognition oozes like honey from who is being mirrored, but I can't remember her name—yet.

With no frame of reference for this early mystical experience, and in a flash of passion for the color blue, I was donning my plaid uniform for the first year of a nearly life-long Catholic school career. I learned how to make the Sign of the Cross, create Crayola renderings of baby Jesus in the manger (replete with a twinkling Star of Bethlehem); followed months later by his crucifixion and a weeping Mary. When the assignment was to draw God, I promptly drew the parish's Father Don McLaughlin with his silver hair and warm, smiling eyes. God, I thought, was a very nice man.

Still, as the years unfolded, my hunger for communion with this *something-more* experience only deepened into an ever-present ache that hummed a tune I could almost hear. Especially during Mass, creatively cloistering became a survival technique of mine. In trance-like unison, every time the congregation recited: "Lord I am not worthy to receive you but only say the word and I shall be healed." I never knew whether to laugh or cry so I checked out. And then, during one altar-boys-only show, it happened. Someone *within* me had enough identity separation. For a moment, my deep ache collided in breathtaking relationship with the loving reality of her presence. All I could feel was: *I want to go home.*

Like a starlet starving for her big-break, I began chasing the feeling of home and my true identity. This insatiable hunger propelled me into a quest for that which was missing—seemingly, out there—just beyond my grasp. By my mid 20s, this catalyzed me to (certified mail) apply for a spot in New York University's Master's Program in Drama Therapy. *Haaaah, yes, I have found it! Cue the happy dance music because this will reveal the role I must play to finally become—myself.*

It's okay. You can chuckle, too.

Upon acceptance, head-first, I dived into all manner of study that ran the gamut from Abnormal Psychology to Psychodrama. And I loved it. Well into the evenings, my classmates and I came together to tell our stories, reverse roles and cry like we were being witnessed rather than watched. I was happy to be a pioneering soldier willing to answer the question, "what is drama therapy" for the rest of my life.

However, as the semesters played out, something began to gnaw at that all-too-familiar ache and, to be honest, my overall well-being. The harder I pushed, tried, worked and gave, the more self-abandoned and separated I became. Exactly when, *oh when*, will I embody this elusive and transformative role that will, once-and-for-all, allow me to become myself?

Hello, internship time. I'm the novice working on an in-patient psychiatric unit with children who are suicidal, homicidal or both. It's not an easy assignment but I adore the trenches. My thesis centers on 12 patients who I am guiding to play the role of God and, in turn, access their own healer. Amidst cackling nurses threatening restraints and quiet rooms, grace infuses the air as each patient embodies God.

A wise and loving voice was closely present *through every child* regardless of whether they had — days before — threatened their wheel-chair bound grandmother with a glass bottle, tried to microwave the family kitten or sliced their own arm after being raped. My final session complete, it's Christmas Eve, and my last day on the unit. As the clock strikes three, I am ushered through the heavy door. "Don't worry," says the resident drama therapist. "It will get easier."

"I feel like I'm *dying!*" I say to my mother, less than one month later, waving my hands as though they've caught fire. "I don't know who I am." There's no formal diagnosis called Soul-Loss, yet it's a pervasively modern epidemic that I was beginning to recover from. But let me tell you, this was an agonizing descent into one hell of an experience. While I had no prior psychiatric history, doctors declared I was suffering from a major depressive episode. My parents boldly asserted this was my Dark Night of the Soul — and thank God they did.

In the meantime, I cannot get out of bed or form coherent sentences. Lifting my little dog, Jem, onto my bed is the movement of the day. Self-protective strategies (or roles) begin peeling away. My life, as I knew it, spectacularly crumbles. It felt like my beloved God had cruelly abandoned me in a Twilight Zone so distant; Rod Serling wouldn't visit. I didn't think it was possible to feel such human *nothingness* yet still breathe.

The creeping notion of becoming a patient in a psychiatric unit has been my absolute worst fear since these "symptoms" first appeared. A spiritual emergency was ultimately addressed as a solely medical one. I must say, the moment they handed me hospital gowns was excruciating in its nothingness. Hard as I tried, and despite the loving support of family and friends, this role reversal became official. Devoid of meaning, I have never felt more alone. *God where are you?*

Not unlike the tireless quest to see the Wizard, I remain convinced if I sit with my professor or therapist or friend — anyone but myself — then I'll be okay. Nothing is helping and I'm not getting better. Weeks later, I find myself kneeling before a grotto housing a statue of Mary dressed in blue. I've passed her more times than I can count because this is the Catholic schoolyard of my childhood. With no other soul in sight, I place my hand in hers. I hear a voice within me say, "Give it all to me. It is time."

In the following days, I am called to be still—and *listen* hard. Just like one of the children I guided for my thesis, I start asking God questions and writing down the answers. Slowly I begin sitting up, getting out of bed, talking normally, eating, smiling, laughing—feeling. It's been a long four months. "Surrender and I'll emerge," said this voice within, as the fragrant scent of Penhaligon's Bluebell permeated the air. "You are not alone." It was Easter morning.

The doctor called my spontaneous recovery "remarkable" and "miraculous." Yes, it was, and so much more. The voice speaking all along was not male and certainly not out there. This voice was lyrical, personal and—increasingly *feminine*. And she was engaging from *within* me. Surrender followed by listening, receptivity and a fierce willingness to participate: These are the practices continually leading me home. Like an *at-last* alignment of consciousness, her wise whispers are the soothing elixir I crave. On every level, she is who I yearn to become. She holds my truest emerging story. She's my patient (and I mean *patient*) loving mentor unconditionally related to what's real. So, who is this one? Exactly who healed, rescued, discovered and saved me? Well, I call her my own Blue Feminine Co-Creative Soul—or Blue for short.

The years since my Dark Night of the Soul have been revealing. As a licensed psychotherapist who specializes in transformative coaching, I am humbly aware of the various "issues" caused by separation from our feminine soul—our divine identity. Transformative *co-creative* power is unleashed upon reunion. Better yet, from my soul to yours, allow me to share these love notes:

> *Our majesty transmits in who she's being when surrendered.*

> *We're the quality of attention and presence she's longed for—*
> *"The One" she projected outside herself and, then, wondered why*
> *finding love is hard.*

> *He's our mirror not our source.*

Stop giving him—or anyone else—the credit for who we really are.

Playing the martyr is so last century.

The audition is over and the desire diet, too.

Our dialogues are the answers.

No longer can she afford to keep us waiting in the wings.

That exquisite feeling is us.

She is forever our awakening beauty.

The yearning was mutual.

Let's commit, and recommit, to the un-manifest.

Allow outer life to organize around inner reunion.

It's time to come home.

We are the source of her true identity.

This is an evolutionary relationship authentic

as Judy Garland's final take of "Over the Rainbow."

And wait!

A final word from the original feminine co-creator:

"Feel yourself as God," he would say. *"Feel yourself as God's energy knowing itself. Worship another? Not above thyself but as thyself."*

~Mary Magdalene

Jody Mello

Jody Mello is a Certified Holistic Health Coach, 500 hr Certified Yoga Instructor, Meditation Teacher and Certified Reiki Practitioner. Her passion is empowering other women to heal themselves from the inside out by diving deep into their soul and healing the root cause of their health and emotional issues. After healing her own health and emotional issues holistically, including PTSD, anxiety, depression, disordered eating and pelvic issues, she aims to support other women to truly heal and love themselves on a deep level. She works with women who have a past history of sexual trauma that are experiencing health or emotional eating issues that wish to heal holistically on a deep spiritual level.

🏠 www.nourishedself.com

f www.Facebook.com/NourishedSelf

🐦 www.twitter.com/nourished_self

▶ www.youtube.com/nourishedself

CHAPTER 16

Journey to Self Love: How I Reclaimed My Mind, Body, Spirit and Personal Power.

By Jody Mello

༒

Growing up, I wanted to be a successful, independent, powerful, intelligent woman and carve my own unique path in the world, not be saved by some fairytale prince. I had dreams of curing cancer while also being a dancer. At the same time I secretly found it difficult to love and accept myself. Along my path, I ended up on a detour and stuck in a cycle of dependence, self-hate and self-destruction. This is my story of how I reclaimed my mind, body, spirit and personal power.

At one point in my life I suffered from PTSD, self punishment, disordered eating, anxiety, depression, addictions to sugar and other things, body hate, negative thinking, victimhood and disempowerment, binge drinking, over-exercise, over-work, panic attacks, extreme fear, chronic stress, lack of love, lack of self respect and more.

When I was 18, a ride with my boyfriend's friend ended in rape. As I floated above my body that night, watching everything unfold, feeling helpless, my power was stripped from me, my trust in both myself and others was incredibly shattered and I was left feeling broken. This incident, coupled with another unwanted sexual encounter, and another attempted assault and threats right before I turned 30 left some intense physical, emotional and spiritual wounds for me to heal.

I hit rock bottom when I was so riddled with panic attacks and PTSD symptoms, I was unable to care for myself or earn a living doing what I loved. I couldn't sleep, eat, step outside to do "normal things", make rational decisions for myself or be a loving and nurturing girlfriend or friend. Having a few moments of rest and ease or closing my eyes without freaking out was unheard of. A diagnosis of carcinoma in situ of my cervix and a traumatizing surgery was the icing on the cake. Simple tasks like leaving the apartment to hop on the subway to go to work, or doing the laundry or shopping for groceries were impossible tasks for me. My days were spent in frantic panic attacks, intense fear and incredible fits of shaking and crying uncontrollably. I was a prisoner in my own mind, body and apartment, and I eventually had to take a leave of absence from my job in order to heal myself.

I felt disempowered in every area of my life: career, health, mind, body, relationships, finances and the world. I was 30 years old and unable to function. I went from a strong, independent, successful, intelligent woman to suddenly unable to do the simplest things for myself. I became completely dependent, which was my biggest fear, and the worst feeling in the world. I felt like a failure. After all, I had taken self-defense classes as a teen, I had been "prepared" to protect and defend myself as a girl, yet, I had failed. I felt that I had let everyone down, including myself. I sat crumbled in guilt and shame, as my worst nightmares came true.

The world felt like it was closing in on me, that everything was going wrong and spiraling out of control, that everyone was out to hurt me, that I couldn't speak up out of fear, that I was supposed to just "suck it up" and put on a brave face and that if I really said what I needed to say, I would hear "I told you so", be punished, or felt sorry for. When I found the courage to speak out and seek help, I didn't get what I needed. I fell victim to every circumstance and I had no idea how to crawl out of the mess I had found myself in. I felt like I had been swallowed into a black hole; powerless, consumed by fear, guilt and shame. I felt lost, and so very, very alone.

I turned to traditional medicine out of panic, being handed medication after medication. The side effects were horrendous, therapy wasn't working, and anything I did according to what I "should" do, didn't feel right, so I took my healing into my own hands. I refused to rely on medications to function or feel that I had to "wait and see" if full blown cervical cancer would develop in the next 5-10 years. I was going to do everything I could to take my health and my life back. Every moment I was relying on medications to function, succumbed by fear and not living my life, I was giving my power away to my circumstances. So, I decided to take a different approach to healing.

I pulled out my yoga mat, something I had only used a couple of times, rolled it open, sat down, placed my hands in prayer position, cried and prayed. I'm not religious, but I am spiritual and I do believe in angels and a higher power. I prayed to be led on a path to healing, to regain my health and my life. I prayed to find the courage to do whatever I needed to do in order to heal. I cried tears of pain, sorrow and surrender. I had nothing to lose, so I surrendered to the universe and asked for guidance.

I set a powerful intention that day on my mat and I trusted. I trusted that whatever I needed would be shown to me. I set the intention to heal myself and a whole new world opened up for me. Ask and you shall receive. I am grateful I had the courage to ask for healing, as it led me down an incredible journey that I am now grateful to be able to share with others.

Step by step I made changes. I did the work. I walked through the fire and I healed myself from the inside out. It wasn't easy and it didn't look like I had planned, but it worked. I'll be honest, at one point I wanted to die. The emotional pain was so much to bear that I wasn't sure I would make it through, but I did, and I'm grateful that I'm here to show that healing is possible.

As my body slowly began to unravel and release long held tension, emotions and stories held deep in the cells, I also released my fears, thoughts, experiences, energy and beliefs that no longer served me. The more I was able to release fear, the more I was able to let love in. The more I loved myself from the inside out, the more I was able to heal. The more I was able to create a sense of love, safety and belonging within my own mind and body, the more I was able to move forward.

The universe will keep sending you what you need to heal, until you do. Teachers are always being sent to you if you cultivate this awareness. Learning to stand in my power, speak my voice and forgive and send love to both myself, and others that have harmed me, has been my challenge. I have met it with strength, wisdom and empowerment. For me, there came a time where I began to feel so connected with everyone and I saw myself in every person, even those that had hurt me. There is a saying that every act is either an act of love or a call for love. I knew in my heart that for me to heal and move on, I needed to forgive and let go. The more I held onto anger, the more it tainted my mind, body and life and the more it would eat me up inside, like a slowly growing cancer. The more I could let go, the more I would heal.

I sit humbled at my journey, truly grateful to have healed and to have released the shame and fear. The cervical issues are gone, I now eat in a way that is health promoting, pleasurable and mindful and I no longer turn to unhealthy habits to deal with my emotions or life. I sit in meditation each day as a commitment to myself. I eat clean, move my body to show love and respect as well as healing and I choose empowering and loving thoughts and actions.

Everyone has their obstacles and challenges and I truly believe things happen for you, not to you. We are all here to learn and grow. We have the ability to create, manifest and attract what we want, however, sometimes things are meant just for us, in order to serve the world in our own special way. I feel grateful and blessed.

Our greatest wound is often the place where we can best serve others. I am honored to empower other women who have also experienced sexual trauma to heal their minds, bodies and hearts, take back their health and their lives.

You are not what happened to you. Healing is possible. You just have to say yes to yourself.

"The wound is the place where the light enters you." – Rumi

Rony Reingold, HLC, CPCC

Rony Reingold is the CEO of Embodied Truth Coaching. As a transformational coach, motivational speaker, author and Inspirational Change Agent, Rony works with people who are ready to claim their lives to create more freedom, purpose and unabashed, authentic joy on a daily basis. Rony has guided countless people around the world towards inner and outer success by empowering them to actualize their ultimate dream life. Rony is the creator of the *Reignite Your Radiance* retreats and the revolutionary transformational program *ALIGNED*. Her powerful, holistic and heart-felt approach calls people forward to unleash their deepest wisdom and brightest inner light.

- www.ronyreingold.com
- www.facebook.com/ronyreingold
- www.twitter.com/ronyreingold
- www.linkedin.com/in/ronyreingold

CHAPTER 17

When Spirit Called Me Home

By Rony Reingold, HLC, CPCC

❧

I remember leaning over the kitchen counter at my parents' home, so fatigued I couldn't bring myself to stand up straight.

I remember my distended belly; bloated, hard and full of frustration towards myself for looking mistakenly pregnant and unable to zip up my skinny girl jeans.

I remember driving two hours outside of the city to see the beautiful, rustic man I had fallen so deeply for, despite his addiction to the green substance of avoidance.

I remember the $15,000 check I had received for producing the most impressive photo shoot I'd ever managed, and the feeling of "is this all there is" that came with it.

I remember the subtle seduction of abandoning myself for the approval of another — for my family's schedule, friends' preferences, a promising date, a client's timeline, for whatever it took to not rock the boat too substantially.

I remember my really good life. The undeniably blessed, yet fast moving, wine filled, externally oriented, inwardly craving, well-intended life full of loving family, lifelong friendships, easy money, creative projects, morning workouts, sappy movies and the continual searching for answers outside of myself.

I remember the slow, almost unnoticeable, drip of inauthenticity that coursed through my veins; feeding the ever so slight and unsustainable misalignment of my soul's true nature.

And most of all, I remember the moment when spirit changed my life. Beautifully, quietly, brilliantly knocking me down to a place of surrender, tearing away my walls of illusion, calling me forward and opening a sacred door to the magical, unwavering path of soul and light that has brought me home to my embodied truth.

After living a very fortunate, fun and mostly authentic life, my divine wake up call came in the form of full-body health breakdowns that stopped me dead in my tracks, forcing me to nibble a slice of the Divine's humble pie. The Universe called me several times before I finally agreed to pick up the phone. It literally took me collapsing from fatigue (twice) to accept that something I was doing wasn't quite working.

After a year of going to every conventional doctor I could find and receiving vague diagnoses and suggestions, I simply did the only thing I knew how to do. I kept moving forward. In a state of bewilderment, fatigue and frustration, I pushed on in my career and my habitual work-hard-play-hard life, despite experiencing regular bouts of incredible exhaustion, a distended abdomen, alarming mood swings, hair loss, insomnia and the onslaught of over 30 new food sensitivities.

I would sneak out of photo shoots to take secret naps in my car. I pushed myself to go out with friends, succumbing to the first chair at the bar in which I could find to sit. Feeling too embarrassed, lost and disempowered to share my situation openly with people outside my closest inner circle, I allowed the physical fatigue to become exacerbated by the exhaustion of needing to keep up a façade. It wasn't working.

One day in March of 2009, the Divine whispered in my ear. After vulnerably revealing my distended belly to a thoughtful client, I was sent home from an "important" photo shoot to rest. I went home and laid down on my couch, fed-up and angry with the body that was keeping me from being fully engaged in my life. I felt like my wings were clipped and I didn't understand why this was happening to me. What was this all about?

I'll never forget how deeply I slept that afternoon or the degree of peace and clarity with which I awoke. Quiet and still, I experienced an overwhelming love towards my body and conviction for my greatest potential. I was amazed at how resilient my body was, after putting up with all of my antics. My body was incredible, wise and patient; informing me all along that I was slightly off course. I suddenly understood that *I* was the one who needed to change. *I* was being called into something bigger; and if I didn't do whatever it took to seize the life of my dreams, then things wouldn't actualize in the way I longed for deep within.

The Universe had been calling for quite some time. Finally, utterly surrendered, I picked up the phone and listened to its guidance. It was time to own my truth and realign my entire life with it.

What took place over the next few years was a profound and dedicated process of healing, awakening and returning home to my soul's truest nature. My body and intuition became my ultimate GPS system. I discovered that my inner wisdom came in the form of subtle sensations that were easy to miss if I moved too fast. As I honored them, I trusted my inner knowing and found myself on a truly incredible path. I became a voracious reader, established a team of holistic healers and was uncompromisingly honest with myself and others.

My dreams became non-negotiable. Inspired and committed, I changed my career, dated only men who wanted the family and life I craved, slept in, spoke up, inserted my needs and relearned how to live in my tender and awakened body. There were moments that required immense self-trust, discipline and patience; as well as, moments of fear and prayer. With every conscious choice, I blossomed further. Soon, I was more vibrant and aligned than I was burnt out. I educated my loved ones about my healing process, ditched toxic friendships and shed my stories of being helpless and not enough. I befriended my gremlins, danced with the moon, unleashed my true voice and transcended beyond my physical form. By answering the Divine's call, I claimed the divine in me.

The steady emergence of my truth involved shifting my victim's perspective, where things in life just happen, to a consciousness of radical responsibility, where I recognize that my external reality is a reflection of my inner landscape. Being in partnership with the Divine meant replacing the flashy, "almost right" things in my life with the illuminated, clear YES's. The Divine called on me to outgrow impulsive gratification; and sit instead, with simultaneous discomfort, rightness and internal stillness.

This is a sacred journey and a daily practice of staying home within ourselves. It's a path that requires risking our familiar smallness for the sake of our magnificent and untapped potential. It's about the power of surrender, the glory of opening and the courage to realign ourselves at each new layer of growth. This divine path offers the sweet liberation of authenticity and the empowerment that comes from being intentional and standing in our highest integrity.

I remember the delicious softness in my belly when I realized the man, who is now my husband, was my soul partner on this sacred path.

I remember the journey of birthing my life's work into the world and how validating, freeing and rewarding it was to offer something greater than myself to others.

I remember the power and glory of my liberated, triumphant and radiant voice the first time I sang to an audience from my truth.

I remember the fulfillment I experienced when my relatives unknowingly confirmed for me that living our truth can only serve to bring more love, wisdom and healing to the family unit.

I remember when I was gifted the understanding that every circumstance, obstacle and curve ball we receive is a teacher and an opportunity to evolve.

In the midst of my profound transformation, the clarity of my dream life emerged and became my North Star: To live a peaceful, deeply joyous and authentically empowered life with my soul partner, our children, families and community. Experiencing simple moments in a nourishing home while engaging in gloriously meaningful, inspired work that evolves our world.

My life today is drenched in the sweetness of this vision. I continue to align with it daily. The lush landscape of my current world was revealed to my former self as she gradually unearthed her power, grace and soul's true capacity. I'm deeply grateful for the woman I used to be because she proved to me how perseverant, strong and capable I am. I will always know that about myself thanks to her choice to step into her divine nature.

What pulses through my veins now are courage, light, joy, truth, unwavering commitment and love. It takes humility and vulnerability to stand our ground and live from our truth in the face of all we cannot control. It is a radical act to dare and live a life of peace, purpose and fulfillment. I feel utterly aligned.

My life purpose is to joyously and completely embody my truth. By doing so, I give others permission to walk this wild, delicious and divine path with me, if they so choose. Together, we can spread the light that we are inherently and divinely made of. For ourselves, our children and our world.

Katie McDonald

Katie McDonald is a hairstylist, inspirational speaker and author. She is a single mother of two beautiful children, Declan and Adaline. Katie lives in Denver, Colorado. She enjoys meditating, writing her memoirs and spending time with her family and friends. Katie's vision is to share her story of sexual abuse and empower woman to break their silence and get to work on forgiveness and release. Katie is working as an agent of love, planting seeds of hope through telling her story of healing and transformation. She gives other people permission to do the same in themselves.

CHAPTER 18

My Rose Colored Glasses Shattered – Healing Was My Only Option

By Katie McDonald

༒

I was seven years old the first time I could remember his hand covering my mouth, as his other hand touched me. I was four years old when this happened to me. I immediately thought I had dreamt this. There was no way this could have, actually, happened. I spent the next ten years, ignoring the awful image that was etched in my mind. I desperately wanted affection, from just about anyone who would give it to me. I began a pattern of rejecting real love, in search of impossible love.

When I was seventeen years old, I decided to ask someone in my family if they were touched by the same teenage babysitter. "Yes!!" they said. I remember this wave of relief rushing throughout my entire body. I thought to myself, "I didn't make this up." This had really happened. That day, in that moment, I unconsciously put on rose-colored glasses to protect myself from the pain of this newly discovered reality. They came in handy, especially when times were tough. My glasses provided a form of protection from unpleasant experiences and emotions.

When I was 32 years old, my rose-colored glasses shattered. My life, as I knew it, would forever be changed. It was the morning of February 8th 2013. I was running around trying to get myself, and my son and daughter ready for the day. My son was five and a half, and my daughter was three and a half. Like most days, I was trying to get the kids bathed, dressed and fed with as few tantrums as possible. My daughter was in the bathtub, as I tried to get ready, while yelling for my son to get dressed. Surprisingly, my daughter says, "Mama, we aren't supposed to kiss with our tongues?" I asked her from where she had heard that. I braced myself waiting for her response. What she told me, would forever change our lives.

"Mama, the 15-year-old boy at day care kissed me with his tongue."

"WHAT???!!!! I thought in my head.

I kneeled down beside her, feeling a sense of calmness come over me. I felt myself smile. It was like someone, outside of my body, was making me react this way. She continued to tell me what happened, and I told her that he had made a bad choice. I told her how brave she was for telling me, and that she did the right thing by letting me know. I was here to protect her.

I immediately texted my daycare provider and told her that it was extremely important to call me. I wrote a letter to her, detailing that something serious had happened between our families. When she finally got back to me, I told her what my daughter had told me. At first she said, "no way, are you sure she didn't see that on tv?" I told her that I believed my daughter, and that she needed to figure out what had occurred. She returned my call, crying hysterically. She said that her son had admitted to the act. I was relieved that he had told the truth. I told her we were never coming back. She understood. We both sat on the phone and cried. This was the last time I would speak to her.

For the next six weeks, I experienced emotions and physical pain I never knew existed. Everyone I shared my daughter's story with urged me to call the police or Child Protective Services. I could see the anger in their faces. Why didn't I feel that? Instead, I was numb. I felt immense sadness for my daughter. I hated that this had happened to her. In the same breath, her courage was so beautiful to witness. She had known the act was wrong and had told me. As a result, I could protect and console her.

I was worried about my friend/daycare provider. I didn't want her to get into trouble. I wanted to believe that she was getting her son help. I wanted to believe that she had told the other mothers what had happened.

During this time, my body started to develop a rash. I called my friend who does energy work and told her what had happened. She told me that rashes are supressed rage. Rage? I was upset, but rage wasn't a feeling with which I was familiar.

My rash was getting worse. Every day I would wake up and notice more spots. I was having, what I like to refer to as "hulk moments". The slightest upset would send me over the edge. Who was I? What was happening to me? I realized that something needed to change. My best friend confirmed this after reminding me that I couldn't be responsible for everyone else's wellbeing. I needed to do the right thing for my daughter and this young man. This meant calling Child Protective Services. My therapist made the call for me. I pray that he gets the help he needs and has a chance at a better life.

Adaline was evaluated, and her strength and courage inspired me to break my silence surrounding what had happened to me. I made an appointment with my therapist to finally heal from my abuse.

I sat there. I didn't want to think about it. I was so afraid. I felt like a small child looking under my bed for monsters. I logically know there are no monsters, but my body was anticipating their scary teeth and claws ready to eat me the minute I peeked under. I felt my body tremble. I wanted to leap out of my chair and run for the door.

The truth was, I couldn't run anymore. I had been running all my life. Sprinting away from feeling the pain of what had happened to me that day. My spirit called out to me saying, "Please look at this. Feel this. You deserve to release what happened to you from your mind, body and spirit. This is no longer serving your highest self. I promise you'll be okay. You are safe."

"Tina, I don't want to look at this. It feels like I am back in my bedroom. I feel my bed beneath me. My head is at the foot of my bed. What is he doing with me? I could see myself laying there. I looked down and saw his hand. It was touching me; his other hand over my mouth. I froze. I couldn't do anything. I didn't do anything. My spirit left my body.

I opened my eyes and I was aware of the surrounding of my therapist's office. I felt an overwhelming feeling of filth all over my body. All I wanted to do was wipe off my entire body. I started wiping my arms, starting at the top, and then moving onto my legs. I couldn't get it off fast enough. I just kept wiping. I walked over to the window and brushed off all the disgusting energy that wasn't mine. I wanted to remove it and get it out of my space.

I sat back down in the chair, after doing this for five minutes, or so. Now, I was pissed. How could he have done that to a child? How dare him! \I was so angry. Tina was pleased with my reaction. She kept encouraging me to feel and express what was going on inside my head. She validated my emotions and guided me through this process. She informed me that by bringing this memory to the surface, I was able to see it, feel it and release it. The filth was not mine anymore. I had wiped myself completely clean.

I sat there in the essence of who I truly was. I loved this feeling. For the first time in my life, I knew that this feeling would always be there. That it had been with me all along. I just couldn't see or feel it. I had an obstruction blocking my view of who I was and who we all are.

I feel safe to be in my body once again. I can stay here forever. I am, now, surrounded by unconditional love and support. And I can finally feel it, in its entirety. Wow!

I am so grateful for my daughter who gave me the courage to do this work. I can now stand in my authenticity for my children and for anyone I encounter; giving them permission to do the same for themselves. I don't think I will be needing my rose-colored glasses anymore to protect me from pain. I have God's lenses to see through now.

Michele Semerit Strachan MD

Michele Semerit Strachan, MD has, for thirty years, created a space for the human spirit in medicine. She loves shedding the "doctor" identity and revealing who she is as a healer of the spirit and witness to the miracle of the body. She enjoys an active integrative medicine coaching practice; and has recently created *Connecting Art to Heart*, a rejuvenating program where professional women are encouraged to risk painting in order to reconnect to the vitality of their authentic heart. She is a fellow and the Director of Medicine at the Cultural Wellness Center in Minneapolis.

🏠 **www.askdrstrachan.com**

f **Semerit Strachan**

in **Semerit Strachan**

✉ **dr.semerit@gmail.com**

121

CHAPTER 19

Choosing Me

By Michele Semerit Strachan MD

I am a griot, as my Elders have seen in me, and have named me.

I am the griot of medicine. As I sit quietly in the rooms where people come to tell me their tales of woe and suffering, it is the song of their cells that I hear. I hear the story of spirit inhabiting matter. I move within the story of matter, navigating the marriage with Spirit who penetrates her. Those are the stories I hear; and these are the stories I tell.

It all began with a relentless, hidden, terrifying drive to be chosen. Let me tell you that particular story.

I was born on the island of Haiti where my idyllic memories are of a mystical vibrant place of dance, color and pungent smells. When people ask me, "You don't do life in pastels, do you," it is these images that come to life for me as I silently respond *not even close!*

Coffee is roasting in the backyard, as blue dawn eases the black of night from the sky. Periodically, with the rains, the river angrily roars and takes away portions of the wall tenuously demarcating the boundaries of our land. The days of cutting the grass—grown as tall as children— are hot and magical, filled with the buzzing of gnats and flies and the green smell of hot cut grass.

One day, the Duvalier dictatorship toppled into that childhood. My parents did not come home. They were stopped on the side of the road and taken away to Fort Dimanche, a place where dissidents were locked and suffered unspeakable things. Would we ever see them again?

In a dreadful silence, we were taken to my grandmother's home. When, after weeks, my parents were released, the silence did not relent. Unable to return to their former selves, they decided that they would leave the country. "You can only take one child!" the cruel rules screamed. My parents did not take me.

In that moment, I came to a dreadful conclusion. *You don't have to know what you did wrong.* You might even have done things too right. But you never know when the flaw hidden inside of you will result in your not being chosen. This conclusion would lay buried like a festering infection, shaping my world in catastrophic ways.

Meanwhile, the pieces of my world and how it had been held together lay strewn about me. I have been fascinated by fragments and their relationship between the visible and invisible, ever since.

Five years after medical school, I was to meet the mettle of the test hidden in that childhood day. I was tested and felt I lost it all.

It was a weekend, and as a young, idealistic physician, I had worked the Emergency Room after a long week of regular duties in the clinic. I had tended a particular patient every day beginning Friday evening through Sunday Afternoon. And Monday afternoon found me standing, frozen, along the walls of the passageway that separated our clinic from the more modern part of the hospital. I had been there all morning, feeling the bile in my throat, the roiling nausea in my stomach, the fear clenching my breast bone, the sweat lining my palms. And when the knowledge finally came, no one had to tell me. I just knew the baby was dead.

Ten months old. A baby boy whom I had known since birth, ten months of caring for him as his pediatrician, ten months of shepherding his teen mother into mothering; and now after three days of thinking, assessing, making decisions, and not making other ones, he was gone. He now lay dead in an operating room where the operation had come too late. I had made the wrong diagnosis.

The darkness I entered that day was cold, numbing and terrifying. Questions assailed me day and night: *I had made the mistake, and I was alive. Why?* Had my caring and sensitivity somehow made me too subjective and incompetent as a physician? Or worse, had I failed to truly connect to my patient and his mother? What crucial communication had I been too arrogant, too tired, or too distracted to receive?

I drove myself crazy, fearing that even my preoccupation with these questions was inexcusably self-indulgent, compared to what the other family had to live through. There was no relief, no exit, no permissible reprieve. I worked. I exercised to the point of numbness. I slept until nightmares woke me. I lived in terror and exhaustion.

This time the fragments seemed impossibly flung apart. Yet since I was the one left alive, I did have the task of painfully knitting them together again.

First, the work led me to enter and surrender to a spiritual container: *What does it mean, daily, to dive into the mystery of life, to be grateful for it while knowing deeply that we do not deserve or earn it?* Then I had to wrestle with while a doctor-knowing a lot about life, death, conditions and remedies, I am not God. A power greater than my knowledge and thinking exercised the actuality and timing of life and death.

I grew in this spirituality and humility that was to mark my way and practice. My patients and students appreciated this trademark that characterized me. Yet, the weight of that day would not lift. My heart was still heavy and broken.

One ordinary day, as sometimes transformation happens; I was led inwardly to a point so full of shame and vulnerability, it made me gasp. In glaring clarity, I saw the part of that weekend hidden from me for so many years. When I ruthlessly examined why I had not consulted other physicians, or asked for help as I saw the baby over so many days, I had to face that I had been afraid of what they would think of me, or whether they would judge me as stupid and incompetent. I was also led to look beyond the gasp and shame, and see a thinly-veiled repeat of a little girl afraid that she would not be good enough. A girl who did not know how to be good enough to be chosen by her daddy. She carried in her cells a sense that she might die if he didn't choose her.

In that open exposure, the juxtaposition of my unspeakable fault and innocence looked at me unflinchingly. And, paradoxically, I began to get free. The fragments finally began their self-healing process. It was a process I would follow rather than design.

One day, I met a couple of African elders who introduced me to the work that they had been doing over the previous twenty years. I was initiated into the consciousness of my thinking. This particular cognition—seeing the symbolic value of things and interpenetrating layers of life—was anchored in an ancient African knowledge-spirituality from which not only I, but African people worldwide, have been separated.

Through community building work and the teachings, I was able to revisit that fateful day, in my early career, from the point of view of realizing how much the brutal medical training had separated me from the still inner voice that guides my way of knowing. I began to see the internal exile from my people's spiritual philosophy, reflected in the external events of separation, abandonment and exiles of my early life. I became steeped in an ancestral way of hearing the body and its way of expressing the wounds of our inner life.

I became receptive to the body's wisdom in guiding us, condition by condition; to heal the early wounds in order to emerge into the full-blossoming of unique lessons we have come here to learn by teaching it to others. I learned—and continue to learn—that my unique purpose would return me to the scene of my deepest pain and shame in the world of medicine.

There is a power in bringing the dispersed fragments of self into visibility and symbolic, verbal expression. There is a healing that comes from accepting, dialoguing and giving loving attention to those spurned fragments. But, we cannot accomplish this without community to hold and support us.

My vision is of a place where patient and practitioner—always in touch with vulnerable subjectivity—learn from each other what the fragments feel like, how to find them and what process can enact the reclaiming, re-story-ing and rearranging of them into new patterns of raw beauty and strength in partnership with body.

Angela Rocchio

Angela Rocchio, certified health coach, yoga instructor and empowerment mentor, is committed to creating more happiness on the planet by empowering women to step into their infinite power and wisdom. Angela shares her intimate story of struggle, self-discovery and self-love in the hopes of inspiring women to rise up and live the life they desire and deserve. As a coach and mentor, Angela is dedicated to creating a safe and supportive space for women trying to conceive or who have experienced miscarriage. She helps women reclaim their bodies, heal, manage stress and love themselves.

🏠 http://angelarocchio.com

✉ angela@angelarocchio.com

f www.facebook.com/angelaandthelifttransformation

ⓟ www.pinterest.com/powerandpurpose/

CHAPTER 20

The Journey to Reclaim My Spirit!

By Angela Rocchio

❦

Five years ago, I started on an epic journey. What I thought was a journey to heal my physical body turned out to be something much more powerful and beyond my wildest dreams.

I was approaching thirty and about to marry the man of my dreams. I have to admit our life was pretty amazing living on the coast of California. However, I was struggling from chronic health issues that were compromising my quality of life. Severe allergies, made it impossible to breathe through my nose, taste or smell for months at a time. Poor digestion lead to daily discomfort, food sensitivities and a severe malabsorption of nutrients. The pain and irritability of psoriasis plagued me daily. I was borderline hypothyroid and hypoglycemia. All this left me exhausted, making it hard to enjoy my life fully.

I was very active and ate extremely healthy, so why was this happening to me? Victim feelings aside, I was determined to get to the bottom of it and heal myself naturally. I spent the next year or so, seeing many practitioners of various types of medicine. I tried every elimination diet, going weeks at a time eating only vegetables and the entire year with no sugar, grains or dairy.

Years later and after several diagnoses, I finally found an answer that resonated with me. I had the most severe stage of adrenal fatigue.

Adrenals are responsible for releasing certain hormones that help the body regulate stress. My overworked adrenals were not allowing my body to heal from stress properly. If this hormone imbalance is left untreated for years it can wreak havoc on major processes of the body.

This was my big wake up call. And the funny thing was, once I really grasped that stress was the root cause of my health issues, it didn't surprise me. My intuition had been saying it all along. When I look back in my journals from the past decade, it was a common theme, sometimes written in all capital letters: SLOW DOWN. I didn't listen and kept going about my fast-paced lifestyle.

I had become unknowingly infatuated with stress and staying incessantly busy. My daily focus was on how much I could accomplish. The dialogue going on in my head argued that if I didn't accomplish my to-do list, I was lazy or wasting time. I was extremely productive, but that came with a price. My addiction to this fast-paced lifestyle was destroying my nervous system and making me physically sick. Either I could keep going along this path of compromised health, taking medication for the rest of my life, or I could learn to slow down and heal my body.

Where did this fast-paced mentality come from to begin with? As I look back on my childhood, one of my earliest memories was of a confident little girl, with a powerful spirit and an authentic passion for life. This confidence and power felt so foreign to me now. I was starving for that feeling and wondered why it left in the first place. Where did that confident girl go?

As I start to dig deeper into the life of that little girl, I start to feel a flood of emotions wash over me; shame, unworthiness, disappointment and abandonment. With each of these emotions I start to recall certain events and realize where I began to give away my power, spirit and confidence, year after year.

It is obvious these events left a strong impression because I remember them so vividly. First, I recalled the embarrassment I felt from being laughed at as a young girl for pronouncing words wrong, writing letters backwards and getting my numbers mixed up. I was the youngest of three girls; and therefore, less educated than them and their friends. Each time someone laughed at my expense, a bit of my power, confidence, and spirit shielded itself and shrunk.

Then I remembered the story I was told as a young girl about my kindergarten teacher wanting to hold me back as a repeat kindergartener. I was to be held back because I couldn't use scissors, and it seemed I had trouble following directions. I didn't know how to use scissors because my sisters experimented with cutting their own hair, which ended in disaster, so my mother, hid all the scissors in the house. I had trouble following directions because I was nervous about doing the wrong thing and getting made fun of.

I was embarrassed when I heard this story. I saw myself as flawed and unintelligent. Thinking back, my poor heart aches for that little girl who felt so unworthy.

When I was fifteen, my whole world flipped upside down when my parents separated. My father left the only home we ever lived in together. Both of my sisters were away at college, so it was just me and my mother at home. This unexpected and tragic event left me not only dealing with the stress of this trauma, but also with the common stresses of being a teenager. Once again, painful feelings of unworthiness, abandonment and shame surfaced for that little girl. Her heart was broken and it was easier to hide her emotions and learn to be strong, than to face them.

Each of these instances left me with the negative belief that I wasn't good enough. You want to know how I dealt with it? I ignored it. So, those beliefs followed me through high school, college and into my adult life, keeping me small and closed off from people and experiences. It was finally becoming clear that my addiction to stress and incessant doing was a strategy I created to distract myself from dealing with the pain and sadness of my past.

Now, fast forward to a couple years ago when I experienced the most tremendous loss. I had a miscarriage. My husband and I were so excited sitting in the hospital room at our 12-week ultrasound. The doctor started the ultrasound machine and it wasn't long before our excitement was crushed with news that the pregnancy was no longer viable, and I would have a miscarriage in the next couple of weeks. Needless to say, we were devastated.

We don't know the exact reason for my miscarriage, but often late miscarriage, which this was considered, is linked to health issues of the mother-to-be. So along with the pain, I felt ashamed and inept. Once again, feelings of not being good enough surfaced.

That was the final straw. I was ready to listen to that voice inside, saying SLOW DOWN. There was nothing like the motivation of longing to be a mother to motivate me towards action. So that's what I did, and that's when the real healing and awakening occurred on a mental, emotional, physical and spiritual level. Through this journey, I not only healed my physical body, I reclaimed my spirit; the spirit of that little girl. That spirit we are all born with.

The situations we endure in this life seem unfair; and on some level, they are. None of us should have had to go through those painful experiences. We truly deserve to be unconditionally loved, respected and celebrated. But the reality is, we have all experienced pain, abuse, neglect or abandonment of some kind.

I know you have a story to share. How has your story shaped you? How can you heal the pain of your past and use it to truly awaken?

Our challenges are opportunities for growth, not meant to be wasted. If we don't embrace our stories we are keeping ourselves from living the life we deserve, one of overwhelming happiness and great health. If we are willing to slow down enough to unearth those stories, listen deeply to their lessons, reframe them and forgive ourselves and others, we will be set free.

I know the pain, struggle and stress of trying to conceive and suffering miscarriage. It is through sharing the most intimate parts of my story that I hope to inspire women to heal and recognize their infinite wisdom and power. I have dedicated my life's work to creating a safe and supportive space for women who are trying to conceive or heal from experiencing miscarriage. I hope to help women manage their stress, while empowering them to love themselves through the process.

Now only months away from giving birth, I feel so blessed for my journey of self-discovery and love. I consider this voyage sacred, as it has prepared me for the ultimate passage to motherhood. Each part of my journey shapes who I am, and has connected me with my life's purpose. For that, I am eternally grateful.

I am no longer living by the negative beliefs of my past; instead, I truly live from my heart. As I live from my heart, I am experiencing life beyond my wildest dreams; and with this, I honor myself, all beings and the Divine Creator.

Stephanie Locricchio, CHHC, ACADP

Stephanie Locricchio is a graduate of the Institute for Integrative Nutrition and is certified by the American Association of Drugless Practitioners. As a multitasking Mompreneur, she wears many hats: licensed esthetician, speaker, writer and food activist. Her mission is to raise awareness on issues that impact health and wellness. Through education, she empowers people to make better choices on food and personal care products. She offers a clean living program which has assisted hundreds in reaching their health goals and recover from food related disorders.

Through her work, Stephanie has built a team of Wellness Warriors on a mission to impact change and create a cleaner, healthier future; proving that there is power in numbers. Together they are assisting others to step into their power to live a prosperous, clean and balanced life.

✉ slocricchio@gmail.com

🏠 www.stephanielocricchio.com

f www.facebook.com/stephanie.locricchio

f www.facebook.com/wellnesswarriorsunite

in Stephanie Locricchio

CHAPTER 21

Better the Pain than to Remain the Same

By Stephanie Locricchio, CHHC, AADP

Transformation, while profound, can be difficult when navigating through the transition. We all have greatness within us. The hope is that while going through our journey, we can find, harness and share our unique gift with the world. Mine has been a lifelong journey filled with peaks and valleys.

I was a very precocious child with strong opinions and a vivacious personality. My school years were filled with torment and isolation. I was a difficult teen who desperately wanted to make my own choices. I often rebelled against authority. In high school, I longed for acceptance and placed value on the quantity of friends versus the quality.

Insecure on the inside, and always seeking approval and validation from outside sources; I spent a large part of my teenage and early adult life trying to please others and never feeling personally fulfilled. Restless in my career and unsettled in my life, I bounced from job to job. An overachiever and my own worst critic, I often beat myself up about never finishing anything I started. I always felt bigger than the role I was in and knew that I was meant to do something great.

I met my husband in my early twenties, and a whirlwind romance led to quick nuptials. The first few years of marriage were tumultuous and filled with conflict. Strong personalities, unrealistic expectations and a battle of wills left us on the verge of divorce. Our commitment to each other and the marriage pulled us through, and we were finally ready to have a family.

The road to pregnancy was difficult; it took over a year to conceive. The moment I saw the positive pregnancy test, I was filled with joy and rushed off to surprise my husband at work. I could not contain my excitement and told everyone the news. At our first sonogram, I was delivered news that no expectant mother wants to ever hear—my pregnancy was not viable. It was a waiting game from that point. A miscarriage was inevitable, so my doctor scheduled a DNC to terminate the pregnancy.

Again, I felt like a failure, and sharing the news with my husband was one of the hardest things I ever had to do. The DNC came and went. I put on my bravest face and life marched on. It was around holiday time, so I was distracted and pushed my feelings of loss aside. I rationalized why something so terrible would happen, and believed there was a reason. Maybe, I needed to focus on my career or maybe it wasn't the time for me to become a mother.

I accepted the loss, moving forward in accepting that motherhood was not in the plan, this time. Shortly after, I discovered I was pregnant again. I was overcome with fear, and mentally prepared myself for another loss. I swore my closest family members to secrecy, and proceeded with caution to my first sonogram appointment. I held my breath the entire time. The news was good. The pregnancy was viable and I heard my son's heartbeat for the first time. That sound was music to my ears.

This moment of joy was quickly interrupted with news that I had a blood clotting disorder that required daily injections and biweekly sonograms. I wasn't a fan of injections, medical interventions or medications, but my motherly instinct kicked in and I was willing to do anything to have a child. Nine long months of scary moments, painful injections, bed rest and constant fear dragged on for what seemed an eternity. Focusing on the amazing gift I was carrying inside kept me going during the really tough times.

Pregnancy is a miracle. You change physically and mentally, the instant the test reads positive. The nine-month period leads to a moment filled with expectations, emotions, fear and joy. A labor of love leads to the moment you are holding your most beautiful creation in your arms. It's at that moment when everything changes and life is forever complicated in the most beautiful and unexpected ways.

I was determined to be Super Mom—high-powered career woman, perfect wife, gourmet chef, housekeeper and nurturer. The joy of my son was followed by anxiety and overwhelmed feelings. I was faced with so many decisions, while exhaustion from the birthing process and physical pain set in. I had to learn the art of breastfeeding, make decisions about vaccines and co-sleeping.

Parenting is demanding from the moment you hear the beautiful cry of your newborn baby passing through your body and into the world. A silent shift from fear to control took place, as I realized that I could no longer protect him from everything. There is no book that could have prepared me for the life changes that came with raising a family.

Besides the full-time demands of motherhood, the clock was ticking. I had twelve weeks to find a new normal before returning to my other full time job. Overwhelmed with schedules, pumping and a touch of postpartum, time passed and I returned to work. Within the first week, I was on a flight to San Francisco—breast pump in tow, tears in my eyes and guilt in my heart. I was truly pulled between two worlds. Consumed with schedules, deadlines and guilt I was exhausted mentally and physically. It was clear that my neat little plan had several holes that could have never been predicted.

Both my family and career required my undivided attention. Busy all day and guilty every night, I was sure that I was messing it all up. I was not present in any part of my life and found myself caught in a viscous cycle of drowning in guilt, anxiety, fear of judgement and failure. It was clearly time to accept that I couldn't do it all. I hesitantly gave my notice and walked away from everything—title, salary, benefits and expense account.

The harsh reality of living on one income set in quickly. Feeling torn and helpless, I bounced from part-time job to part-time job looking for the perfect balance. As crippling blame, frustration and fear robbed me of my joy, I knew it was time to step back and get in touch with my inner compass. The outside world was extremely noisy. There was judgement, mixed messages and shiny objects to distract me from what was right in front of you. Focusing inward brought amazing clarity, and I was called to service.

Being a modern-day mom, I knew, first-hand, the issues we face in the 21st century. Our children have become science experiments for the food and pharmaceutical industries. Thus, I longed for knowledge that would support my parental instincts regarding my family's health. My alternative lifestyle choices were far from mainstream. My instincts differed from my doctor's opinion, and I didn't know which to follow. This thirst for knowledge led me to pursue a career in wellness.

Stepping outside of my comfort zone caused trepidation, but I trusted the process. Living in fear, and my need to control, were no longer serving me. I chose to let go and follow my heart. After graduating and becoming a Certified Health Coach, I linked arms with a like-minded community and found a home with network marketing. I was, finally, designing a life where I no longer had to choose. I had reclaimed my identity, powerful, passionate and inspired. My work served others and shared the knowledge I had from life experiences. I felt alive, as I shared my important message. The fog had lifted and suddenly things were clear again.

Today, I am transforming lives physically and financially through the work I am doing. I am designing a life for my family that I never thought possible. Stepping outside my comfort zone and into the unknown has been the most rewarding experience of my life. Educating, empowering and inspiring others to dream big and live their best life is gratifying on every level.

Life is not about the destination, but enjoying the journey and loving yourself; good, bad or indifferent. Each of us is powerful beyond measure, and it is when we tap into our divine light and share it with the world that the amazing ride, called life, truly begins.

Be authentically you and stay true to your vision, values and passion. Quiet the mind and hear the voice inside that tells you where to go and how to get there. The road is paved with unexpected twists and turns along the way. Never let fear deter you from dreaming big and working toward the life you deserve. It is the pain of change that assists us in reaching our full potential. In the words of Paulo Coelho, "We all know fear but passion makes us fearless."

Lindsay Hinton

Lindsay Hinton is an Intuitive Strategist and Consultant, author, speaker, spiritual mentor and retreat facilitator working with powerhouse awakening women and soul-inspired entrepreneurs to bring their fullest vision of life and business into fruition. She and her business partner, Kate Fehr, facilitate a unique and soul-shifting experience for their clients that focuses on bringing their internal and external worlds into full alignment, while building a clear and joyful vision for life so that they can maximize their passion, purpose, and prosperity. She is also the co-creator of *Whole Woman Retreats, Wild Women Workshops* and Soul Inspired Wellness's forthcoming *Wild Community* and *Whole Mama* retreats, all of which are dedicated to restoring people to an authentic, whole, and vibrant life.

CHAPTER 22

Joy Rising

By Lindsay Hinton

For many of us, there is a moment, or several, that we can retrospectively pinpoint as the markers that changed the trajectory of our lives. For others, we don't know exactly where things shifted; just that we are far from the place we expected we would be today.

I was in second grade when the years of violence began. He would smoothly, yet forcefully, swagger toward me, and with a swift and heavy-handed directive, take me around the corner of his house. His forearm would press firmly against my chest until my back met the wall. Then with his free hand, he would assist my pants in meeting the ground. As he did this, my eyes would immediately divert to meet the sky.

I learned, quickly, how to dissociate from my body, so as to not feel the searing pain that soon followed that series of events. I also became a master at connecting to the stillness of the natural world, especially in those moments. The practice of dissociating allowed me to envision myself peacefully soaring high above, like the birds that flew overhead, free from it all, weightless in those very heavy moments.

The birds. I noticed the birds always seemed to show up and watch over me as I endured things no child should have to, but many unfortunately do. To this day, birds still speak to me.

I did not tell a single soul about the abuses for years. I could never find the words or the courage to do so. The violence continued for three long years until one day it stopped, and I was "safe". Born from those events, however, were the patterns that emerged and endured until recently in my life. The generalized fear. The deeply seated insecurity. The distortion in my perception of the masculine was combined with an inability to fully trust men, a deep disconnection from my physical body and an incredibly low sense of self-worth.

In 2011, I was diagnosed with depression, a diagnosis that brought simultaneous relief and disappointment. The blessing was that someone had finally acknowledged aloud that things were out of balance in my life. The painful part was, I'd just become part of a growing statistic in our country. Being labeled with a "mental health diagnosis" was an assault to my ego. This hit me in every vulnerable, internal place. I felt like a failure, something less than, an *other*.

My partner at the time brought to my attention our lack of physical connection. My mind had become quite comfortable rationalizing my lack of sexual appetite and energy, in general, as a result of being a full-time working mama, with two young boys to care for. But as I asked around, my girlfriends all confirmed that they engaged their partners often, thought about it often and liked the joyful and playful experience.

I started to reflect on all of my relationships in which I was intimately involved. I recognized, immediately, that sexual connection was seldom something I desired or felt comfortable with. In fact, sex was often something that made me shut down; as in, sometimes my body would go completely numb. Sexual connection frequently felt like a chore or service I offered, not something I was present in my body for; and certainly not something that brought great pleasure and release as it was designed to do. Though my experience improved, tremendously, with my husband at the time, sex was by no means something I organically desired.

So off I went to therapy. I was committed to doing everything I could to revitalize my marriage and heal and awaken whatever it was that kept me from connecting intimately in this way. As I sat on my therapist's couch trying to save my marriage, my little lady within, the one who was present at that initial abuse, showed up in the process. I mean, literally, showed up in a vision I had, one of the first and most profound visions of my life. That vision became the core of my healing journey and the foundation of my business that was born months later; though at the time, I had no idea about all that was coming.

I realized with great clarity, that while physically I had grown into a woman, emotionally the piece of my psyche that held my experience was left disconnected, afraid, alone and so unsure of herself. She had stayed present with me all along. She never left and she never healed. She was never heard, or honored, or allowed to express in any way the fear, hurt, shame, anger and intensity of those experiences. Instead, I did the best I knew to do. I stuffed all of those emotions deep down inside of me, ignored them and hoped the feelings would dissolve over time. But of course, that is never how it works.

As I began to see her within all of my present day struggle, I felt her energy so clearly, and I quickly recognized that the part of my mind that held her experiences had literally become an energetic black hole in my life. The weight of unresolved emotions had become the storehouse and source of depression, anger, lack of trust, fear and indecision. Her wounds kept calling the experience of pain and abuse, in some form, into my space. And over and over again, I experienced things that reinforced her pain and her perceptions of what life and relationships, especially with men, should look like and feel.

After my recognition of this surfaced, I quickly asked my therapist if we could quit working with my process specifically around the abuse and my abuser, and instead focus our work on integrating my wounded inner child back into my present day experience. We did. As we worked with her, and gave her permission to express herself and heal, I unearthed new and joyful territory within myself. I discovered a vast landscape with depth and color, incredible potential for creative expression, and a source to something wild and timeless, where I could tap into an endless well of wonder and wisdom.

As I began exploring this new space in my internal world, and working through all of the old patterns and emotions that would organically, I moved forward in my intimate world and space. My visions became much more clear and vocal, *literally*.

A few months after I beginning my healing process, I woke up one morning to a voice in my heart that so clearly and powerfully stated, "Start your business." I knew, immediately, that there would be consequences for not honoring that sacred whisper. A social worker at the time, I had no idea what that meant or where to begin, but I responded in kind, "YES! Okay Life, show me the way. I am yours in service."

From there, as if by pure magic, people, experiences, synchronistic events, visions, channeled writings and more began to dominate my space, guiding me to the next right action. The joy just kept rising and expanding. I kept leaning in more and listening, while courageously saying yes to the soul-stirrings and experiences that were calling me. What has unfolded in my life in the past three years has been nothing short of miraculous.

I look back now from the perspective of the Whole Woman I am today—and of course, always was—and I welcome every moment of life. I feel gratitude, hope, strength, resilience, love and forgiveness; and I know that my pain and the patterns that were born from that initial abuse were not in vain. Those experiences were coupled with profound purpose. They liberated me, and were the ultimate gift of transcendence. I honor the love and learning, the breaking open to break through.

Ultimately, what I have learned is that each moment offers us choice. A choice to stay or go, speak truth or hide behind an old story, love or live in fear, rise or stay buried beneath the weight of what was. The painful experiences took me to my depths and facilitated a process of awakening in my life. I chose me. I chose life. My own healing equipped me with greater understanding and insight that brought so much new, empowered life into my world and experiences.

This path allowed me to create radical transformation in my own life, and facilitate that in the lives of my clients. Today, I stand fully present in my life, guided by love and service, opening and receiving; allowing my truth and passions to forge a new pathway. If I had to give my journey a name, it'd be called "Joy Rising."

IN PURSUIT OF THE DIVINE

Chloë Rain

Chloë Rain is a Human Experience Artist, Navigator of Lost Souls, and Nostalgia Poet. Chloë creates visual and literary works of art via divine imagination, igniting powerful healing energies and cleansing emotional responses. Her experience art is set against the backdrop of the mundane, day-to-day human drama. As a professionally trained life coach and natural intuitive, Chloë is highly skilled in provoking massive transformation in those seeking permanent change. She works with conscious leaders and individuals seeking a more integrated spiritual relationship to money, creativity, personal freedom and presence in the new-age, global community.

✉ **purpose@chloerain.com**

⌂ **http://chloerain.com**

⌂ **Creative Retreats: http://chloerain.com/creativevacation**

f **www.facebook.com/ChloeRain**

CHAPTER 23

Risking Everything

By Chloë Rain

ℰ⁄ℴℴ℺

I whispered the fragile secrets cradled deep within my heart. I spoke them in confidence to the ones I trusted, the ones who claimed to love me and support me, only to have my own secrets used against me. The throat-clutching, fearful advice, the screaming, the threats; how could I not listen? How could I go on living a divided life? I was dead inside; and even more frightening, I wished I were dead.

I remember, stone-faced and emotionless, repeating to my mother, as we stood in the driveway, "This is not a life. This is not a way to live. I'm not alive. This is not a life I am living."

"What will you do?" she asked.

"I don't know." I replied. "But I can't go on like this. I'm going to leave."

I remember it was Friday, and I was standing in my heels in my office, holding my cell phone and screaming at the contractor on the other end. I told him to get his act in order or he would suffer the consequences of litigation. As I looked across the room at my assistant sitting in her office, I saw the expression on her face. I saw myself through her eyes.

Putting the phone down, I thought, "I hate myself. I hate the woman I have become."

That was the end for me. Three days later, I sent a brief email resigning from my position with the company. I wrote: *It has become clear to me that I must leave.* And as if in a movie, the response received within moments was: *as you wish.*

Is this the fate of dreamers? Must I risk everything? Could I relinquish all safety and security for the unknown? Must I leave everything I've ever identified myself with in order to find myself?

From where I came, everything made sense. There was security in the mundane. Now, nothing made sense. Why must I risk everything for the one thing that had become more precious than life? *The desire to live.* I wanted to know love. I wanted to have a reason to get out of bed in the morning. I longed for freedom.

When I quit my corporate job after a fifteen-year executive career in real-estate development and insurance sales, I thought that was the hard part. At the time, all I wanted was to fall in love and find a husband; that was all I had wanted for years.

But the way I had approached things, was to become the best *man* I knew how to be. I had lost myself in the hard work. I became hard as nails. I travelled all over the country, regularly working 16-hour days, until my hair started falling out and my body went into all systems fail. Even if I had desired to keep going down the path I was on, there was no way my body was having it. Truthfully, I had become so disconnected from life and desire that I contemplated ending it all, rather than go on the way I was.

I contemplated suicide more than once that year.

One morning in April, I woke up compelled to go to the top of Rattlesnake Ledge. I sat on the edge and dared to dangle my legs looking at the ground, imagining myself at the bottom, sprawled out, dead. I thought I'd probably catch a few trees on the way down and my body would end up in some awkward position and that's how they'd find me. I felt that scene was pretty horrible, and I couldn't bear to think of my family and my friends finding out about me in that way. Yeah, when I really leaned over the edge, fully contemplating the way down and the inevitable landing the long (long) way down, I knew I didn't want to die.

I didn't want to be dead. Okay, that must have meant I wanted to be alive? I sat there and tears dropped down my face, but I didn't sob. I was numb. I wondered if anyone had noticed the girl sitting too close to the edge, and if they realized I was making a go of it.

If I was going to keep living, I had to figure out a way to feel alive. I wanted my life to have feeling and purpose. I wanted to fall in love. I wanted to be made love to.

◆ ◆ ◆

Something was very wrong with me, my body was failing, my right arm had become partially paralyzed, and I was still trying to hold it all together. After weeks of blood testing, a certain test came back totally off the charts—red blood cells mutated, antibodies attacking my endocrine system by the thousands. The doctor prescribed immediate hormone therapy. I was nervous taking medication, considering the state I was in and how sensitive I was to any kind of chemical, hormone or drug, etc. I hadn't filled a prescription in over five years.

When I ended up in my acupuncturist's office in a total fog and depressed beyond sanity, Dennis asked me what was going on, very concerned about how depressed I had become, almost instantly after taking the medication. He asked me to call my doctor immediately. My acupuncturist had become a trusted confidant over the past year, after treating me for anxiety and smoking cessation. He had had faith in me that I would quit smoking, even when I would leave his office and light up. His caring treatment had revealed layers of emotional attachment I had to smoking and disease. Then one day, I just didn't want to light up anymore.

My doctor told me it was a coincidence that I had become suicidal after taking the hormones. So, I fired him. Even if I believed in such things, what an outrageous thing for a doctor to say! I don't believe in coincidences, by the way. There is no such thing as coincidence. I stopped taking the hormone therapy immediately. As the fog lifted, I was able to remember all the reasons I had decided to keep living.

My health had, ultimately, brought me to my knees and led me down the path of self-inquiry, recovery and towards new ways of being in the world. Somehow, I knew (in that way you just know things) when all of it started that part—or maybe the entire purpose—of doing the brave thing was to start the brave conversation. To talk about all of it, share my doubts and longings with others, had to help someone. There had to be others with the same desires. I had to show them another way.

When death was no longer an option because I had come to love myself too much, I stopped listening to all the fear and bad advice, and began to listen to the soft voice within, gently leading me to freedom and bringing me moments of bliss. In other moments, when life didn't seem fair, I thought about all the plans I had made for something different.

Something inside of me had broken— broken open, beyond self-repair. For my entire life, I had suffocated quietly under the guise of having all my shit together. For years, I was embarrassed by my inability to be happy. I was working and trying so hard; and yet, I'd been single and loveless for more years than I was comfortable admitting. I'd never had an adult romance and I had no idea how to ask for the love I needed and desired.

Moreover, I was ashamed by my inability to admit my creative desires. I had been slowing dying inside for years. I had been witness and participant for too long. I had lived in a reality where people didn't say what they mean, we didn't show how we felt and the dark places we find ourselves in were unmentioned. The silence was killing me.

I realized I could no longer return to the life I once led. I could no longer live the life I planned for. I had to embrace the life that was meant for me.

I'm not dead (yet) and death is no longer an option. I know how fortunate I am to be alive. Many have passed, and others are leading internally dead lives. So, I went to seek the thing that had eluded me my entire life: real, bone gripping, earth shaking, happiness. Though I am already *she*, I felt as though I'd just handed my most precious thing to a cloaked stranger that said: "You must let go, in order to go on."

And so I did.

Jodie Rodenbaugh, CPT, CPC, MA Ed

Jodie Rodenbaugh is the Sexy Soul Liberator who holds the key to unlocking your hidden desires. She's armed with a Master's in Education, a background in science and brain research and certifications in Energy Leadership, life coaching, and personal training. She has a lifetime of lost-love experience with intuitive skills of reaching the Truth and natural cause of your setbacks. She's been called to empower men, women and children to live the life they're here to love.

For more Sexy Soul tips, tricks, and love wisdom follow:

🏠 www.sexysoulmakeover.com

🐦 www.twitter.com/sexysoulcoach

📌 www.pinterest.com/jodierodenbaugh/

in www.linkedin.com/in/jodierodenbaugh/

CHAPTER 24

A Beautiful Mess: From Pain to Purpose

By Jodie Rodenbaugh, CPT, CPC, MA Ed

❧

For the first five years of my life, I spent much of my time as a little scientist, curious about the world. I had a deep, inner knowledge that there was always something more than what I saw in front of me—my smile as big as the moon and eyes as bright as the sun told me so. I saw beauty in everything, except for those Hee-Haw overalls my mom made me wear to preschool. I refused to see the beauty in those, and won that battle by getting to quit that school all together. I learned to fight for beauty and I knew God had my back on that one.

From a very early age, I would have visions of a world unknown to us. I always knew there was something more out there. My visions were like dreams, while awake. I would become this tiny, microscopic being and travel to places I'd never been. I remember asking friends if they ever thought like I did, if they ever wondered or imagined that there was a world outside of what we knew. They thought I was crazy.

Then came grief. One bright, sunny day my mom, sister and I were planting flowers with my grandma. She was such a lovely woman with a huge smile and bright eyes. Suddenly, while smiling her brightest smile, she leaned over her deck, falling two stories to her death in front of us. My mom never fully recovered from that loss. Although, I do believe it woke her just enough to recognize she was with the wrong man and headed in a direction she didn't want to go. She divorced my dad just a few years later.

My mom was a beautiful woman in her time, young, bright, stylish and full of faith. She broke free from the drug era of the seventies, and found her identity, instead, in the scent of Channel No. 5, silk blouses and narrow pencil skirts. She worked in accounts payable and had outstanding benefits for our family, which she attributed to the grace of God.

Her faith was strong even though she had a fear of feeling alone. I remember my mom being so afraid of the roads after her thirty-minute commute from work that she would come home crying. But, she would set out to do it all again the next day. She proved those fears by manifesting several major wrecks, but always came out externally unharmed.

She put us through Christian schools until we went to college, and always made sure she had quality food to put on our table. We were poor by many standards, but I honestly don't remember feeling lack. She taught me, at an early age, that money was always there and would be there when we needed it. She'd say, "God always provides when we need it." To me, my mom was the epitome of strength, but I knew I wanted something different for my life.

The theme for the next 20 years was lack of boundaries. I knew that for every problem there must also be a solution. I held strong to this belief.

My mom married my stepdad when I was 12. She thought he was a knight in shining armor, which he did portray himself to be. Things changed rapidly after they got married. He carried significant pain from his childhood and couldn't allow himself to be happy or worthy of love. My mom embraced his pain, thinking she could heal it. But, he became emotionally abusive, a toxic alcoholic, lost his career as a VP at a bank and spent most of his time puking his guts out for hours in the shower.

My stepdad gave us unusual punishment, and yet I loved him. I felt his pain, even as he criticized my mom. I was confused by this relationship, but I knew it wasn't healthy or godly. This was a problem, and I set out to prove the solution—healthy relationships.

At 13, as I collected data while escaping the emotional abuse I witnessed at home, I found myself in a different kind of abuse with my hand being forced onto my friend's father's penis. I remember going inside for a cookie; and the next thing I remember, I'm on the floor with my eyes closed tight and frozen with fear. I felt alone and ashamed for not being able to use my voice and scream what I wanted to say, but I prayed it would end and it did. I was lost after this and my data got skewed in my exploration of boys. It was the darkest three years of my life.

I was often scared as a kid; these were dark days. I rarely slept alone, I wouldn't go to another room in the house by myself and I would stay up most of the night frightened to death that someone else was with me. I would freeze up, wanting to yell out for my mom, but could never get the words out. One of the most painful experiences in life is not being able to speak your words. My mom would always give me a phrase of faith to hold onto.

High school was my saving grace. Those were the years I found myself. I found my identity in cheerleading, friends, science, affirmations, drama, clothing 101 and laughter. I shared lots of laughter with people who were good, who had both parents in their homes, who had high expectations for education and extracurricular activities; and most of all, an undying faith at the forefront of their relationships. I had had amazing relationships with both genders, and I felt I had the data to make a decision on the kind of man I would marry.

By my junior year in high school, I knew exactly what I wanted to do with my life and why I wanted to do it. This reasoning drove me. I wanted to teach and inspire children to go where they were called to go, regardless of where they came from. I had a natural capacity for seeing someone's inner genius and it excited me to use this gift.

After college, I moved in with my boyfriend of three years and we were really good at playing house for the first few months. That's until he decided to bring someone else into our lives. I was devastated, but it taught me to trust my gut, recognize the red flags and use my intuitive gifts.

A year later, I met a boy who wore bright red tennis shoes, a hockey jersey and sat on a bright green Ninja. Not the kind of guy I would have picked in a line up, but he drew me in like a bee to honey. After much debate and sabotage, on my part, I married that man four years later. We had the perfect life from any outside view, a custom-built home, two kids and careers we led in and loved. But on the inside, I was a mess.

I didn't know how to love my husband the way my inner spirit was instructing me to. I had a deep fear of being left alone. I felt stuck, broken as a wife and ashamed for not being able to follow through with how I wanted to love. My husband told me I needed counselling my secret was out. He saw me. I had been studying relationships my entire life. It was time to go deeper and I got laser-focused on loving the way I wanted to love him. I made huge progress and we decided to celebrate, like many do, by having another child.

Life moved on. I would hear the spirit calling, and I listened more attentively. Then, my biggest fear came true. I was fifteen weeks pregnant, had two small children and I was alone. My husband was accidentally killed by a very common medical procedure. I saw myself in an out-of-body experience, looking down at the frozen state of my life. I felt like I had died too. Then, I heard a familiar internal voice say, "Get in your body. You are here for a reason."

In that moment, I decided it was my responsibility to follow this voice always. I decided to love like I had never known love before, live the life I was being called to live and lead my children with the body I'd been given, with the faith in my destiny. My job is to be her, act toward her and to commit to her. She's why I'm here. She is the beauty to be shared with the world.

I didn't know how I was going to take the steps, but I did know who I wanted to be in the beautiful mess called life.

IN PURSUIT OF THE DIVINE

Ashly Rose Wolf

Ashly is a certified health coach, nutrition educator and holistic nutritionist. After suffering from over a decade of disordered eating, low self-confidence and un-diagnosable health issues, she finally realized that she couldn't get the body or life of her dreams by depriving herself of her desires. While studying at Bauman College and the Institute for Integrative Nutrition, Ashly became impassioned to help other women heal, and created *Healthy Sexy Hungry*. She specializes in body image, disordered eating and holistic healing, and believes that every woman deserves to be healthy, love her body, feel confident and live a deliciously fulfilling life.

✉ healthysexyhungry@gmail.com

🏠 www.healthysexyhungry.com

f www.facebook.com/HealthySexyHungry

🐦 www.twitter.com/HlthySxyHngry

📷 @hlthysxyhngry

CHAPTER 25

How My Hunger Set Me Free

By Ashly Rose Wolf

⸻

My biological mom was a drug addicted schizophrenic, and throughout my childhood, I was exposed to numerous traumatic situations. I never doubted my mother's love for me, but the illogical fears she fed me as a child contributed to my deep sense of fear and uncertainty about the world. From a young age, I couldn't control what seeds she planted in my mind but I could control what I put in my body and how food made me feel. So, food became my comforting friend.

My mom died of a drug overdose when I was ten, and from that point on, whenever I experienced something sad or stressful that I wanted to numb, I turned to food. I numbed myself into adolescence and when I did start to feel again the first thing I felt was an overwhelming sense of self-consciousness.

In order to curb these feelings of inadequacy I turned back to my familiar coping mechanism and started bingeing. By the time I was in high school, I had become a ravenous size 12. At that point, food transitioned from my friend to enemy, but I couldn't stop eating. I was constantly hungry; and when I wasn't hungry, I was sleepy and moody. I had trouble staying awake in class; regardless of how much sleep I had the night before. I often had intense headaches, body aches and stomach aches.

I told my family how I had felt, and was taken to a doctor who ran a gamut of tests and pronounced me healthy as a horse. I certainly felt as fat as a horse. But I, definitely, didn't feel healthy. Deep inside, I felt like something was wrong with me, but everyone else just thought I was a hypochondriac. So, how I felt was never validated.

My stomach issues and feelings of fatigue went on, but I ignored them. This continued on and off until I went away to college. In high school, I had been able to control my emotions by self-medicating with food. When I got to college, however, I couldn't numb my feelings anymore. My decade-long dance of disordered eating morphed into a bad cocktail of anorexia and bulimia. But by this time, I had been engaging in these behaviors for so long that I hadn't only become desensitized to them, I relied on them. Self-sabotage, self-loathing and self-abuse had become a part of my identity.

It took a disturbing wake up call to bring me back to reality. I was at the mall one day, halfway through my senior year of college, when I looked in the dressing room mirror and saw my back and hips. They looked skeletal and I could see my bones protruding. This should have felt like a moment of triumph; I was finally as skinny as I had always wanted to be. But, all I felt was sheer panic. I finally had the body I thought I wanted, but I realized that the way I looked on the outside would never solve the emptiness I felt on the inside. My stomach dropped, as I realized that my whole life with food issues had been a Band-Aid covering up a much bigger problem.

My body cried that day, weeping for me to hear her, pleading for love. The vast amounts of love I received from others wasn't enough because I had no love for myself. While I was standing in the dressing room, looking at my bony body, I felt my inner voice wrap herself around me and tell me everything was going to be okay. From that moment on, my life changed forever. That was the day I met self-love and my healing journey began.

It took six months for me to stop purging and another year to stop the cycle of starving and bingeing all together. My healing process was slow, but steady. While I was addressing my physically addictive habits with food, I was also deep in the trenches of recognizing my emotional addictions.

At the age of 23, I got really sick. Even though I wasn't starving, binging or purging anymore, I would double over with stomach pain. My brain function started to rapidly decline and I started to feel like I was going crazy. It was devastating. I had been consciously making the decision to heal. But instead of getting better, I just kept getting worse.

After a few relentless years of seeing doctors and specialists, I found out that I had gluten intolerance, adrenal fatigue and a severe bacterial infection in my small intestines. My digestive system was completely wrecked. Doctors attributed the damage to a combination of stress, gluten intolerance and my eating disorder. I had suspected that my eating disorder played a role in the rapid decline of my health and wasn't shocked to hear that unhealthy behaviors had led to long-term digestive damage. What I *was* shocked to hear was that I had probably had gluten intolerance and adrenal fatigue since childhood. This meant that all of the times I had complained of pain or fatigue growing up were genuine. It hadn't just been in my head.

Even though my healing journey had taken a frustrating new turn, I felt validated for the first time. Once I felt validated, everything changed. I realized that by blaming everything that wasn't right with my life on my weight, I had ignored what was truly weighing me down. Validation brought revelation. I realized my issue was not with weight, but all of the excuses I created out of fear in an attempt to validate myself.

Fear had held such power over my life that I numbed it out in order to ignore it. But after being validated I realized that instead of ignoring fear, I had to embrace it. As I started to embrace and follow my fear, I was led towards my desires. My fear was, literally, showing me where to go. It wanted me to grow beyond the edges of my comfort zone, while showing me what I wanted out of life, who I wanted to be and how I wanted to feel.

And how I felt was HUNGRY! Hungry for more. More experiences, more connections, more nourishment, more health, more adventure, more fun, more fulfillment and more freedom. I had wanted to feel satiated by food because I wanted to feel satiated by life. I had wanted to eat more because I wanted to fill a void that had been buried deep within me. I had cared so deeply about how I looked on the outside because I wanted to feel deeply on the inside. All that time I had been physically restricting myself, all my body had wanted was to indulge in feeling. I had had it all backwards.

Recognizing this was really liberating, but it was also really scary. Blaming my feelings of inadequacy on my weight was no longer an option. I had to start taking responsibility for how I felt physically, emotionally and spiritually. And the only way to start taking responsibility was to heal. I had to heal my relationship with my body and myself. The only way to do that was to heal my relationship with hunger.

When I consciously started to heal my relationship with hunger, I started listening to my inner guide and I honored what she had to say. I was surprised that all she wanted me to do was live on the edge of my comfort zone. My inner guide wanted me to take risks and to learn what internally lit me up. Over time, I noticed a pattern. The more fulfilled I felt, the less I dwelled on food. The less fulfilled I felt, the more obsessive I became about food and my body. Once I started truly living and feeling, my relationship to food transformed. I was no longer overwhelmed by physical hunger for food, instead I craved a full life.

What I want you to know, dear girl, is that in order for you to heal your relationship with yourself, you have to heal your relationship with hunger. Stop fighting, denying and depriving it. Your hunger is a call of nourishment. Just as you feed your body, feeding your desires is the only way to live a truly fulfilled life. Embracing your hunger is what will ultimately heal you. Heal your hunger, learn to trust it; and as one of my favorite authors, Danielle LaPorte says, "your hunger will lead you home."

IN PURSUIT OF THE DIVINE

Penny L. Sampson

Penny L. Sampson, F.I.E.R.C.E Leadership Life-Stylist, Assertiveness & Leadership Trainer + Mentor, motivational speaker and creator of the *F.I.E.R.C.E Leadership Formula* ™, is a behind-the-scene force of nature, who ardently supports introverted entrepreneurs struggling with marketing, publicity and ownership of their leadership style. Infusing her diverse certifications in the holistic, personal growth and leadership arts with her 20 + years' experience with the entertainment/music/fashion industries, she created dynamic leadership trainings that support her diverse clientele in getting visible, vocal, living uncensored and fully expressed. Clients learn to lead their careers, business and lives from center stage, and on their own terms.

🏠 www.pennylsampson.com

✉ info@pennylsampson.com

f www.facebook.com/PennyLSampson

🐦 www.twitter.com/MindfulExistenc

CHAPTER 26

Death of the Ghost and Rise of the Warrior'ess

By Penny L. Sampson

༄༅

Too much noise, too much chatter and screaming; make it stop! The air is sickly sweet, furiously hot and threatening to steal my breath. I can't breathe. The noise, the screaming, where is it coming from? The room is spinning; my legs feel weak. Lay down, just for a moment. Silence the voices, steady yourself and breathe. The screaming is getting louder, the pressure unbearable. Is this what death feels like? I feel small and ashamed, worthless and inadequate. I have given up. It is not safe to be seen, not safe to be me. Be invisible; be the ghost.

Anger is building, panic is easing, chatter is softening, but who is still shouting? I recognize that voice. She is my own inner alpha, crying to be heard. *Get angry*, she shouts. *Dig in! This is NOT the end for you; it is only the beginning!*

Rebirth…

This was the moment when my entire world collapsed, and all the memories of a life filled with fighting for survival, flooded my mind in mere seconds. That day the Ghost died and I was reborn—born of fire and living fully as a Warrior'ess.

By the age of 38, I had lost everything, including my sense of self and value. Or so I thought. As a child, I was vibrant, outspoken, spunky and rebellious, but these were not admirable or acceptable qualities for a young woman in my era. I spent the following 38 years fighting for my soul's survival in a world that didn't support my individuality, free-spirited rebellious nature, strong character, inner artist and/or my Warrior'ess way of being.

I can recall never being enough for my grandparents. As a result, I was chastised, verbally abused and beaten if I spoke out of turn, in spite of the efforts of support made by my parents.

I continued, for the next 38 years, fighting to be *enough* and safe against stereotypes, and conformity. I was fighting to exist in a world with rules and judgments that felt like torture. I learned to live as a Ghost in the Spotlight, restraining my ever-present Warrior'ess nature, releasing it only under duress. I was only being as much of me, as I thought could be accepted by others.

It was not safe to shine brightly, be vocal and exist outside the norm. Inevitably, I became the introverted, lone wolf, rebel superwoman who believed there were no limits to what could be achieved; but I must do it alone. I had to be the Ghost in the Spotlight, never revealing who and what I really was. Life, for me, meant never letting anyone in, honing my chameleon abilities and ensuring that everyone was kept at arm's length. I believed that this was the only way for me to survive and thrive.

At 18, after leaving home to create my own life, I was gifted entrance into the world of music and entertainment via a club where I took my first adult job. This industry afforded me the anonymity and the flexibility that I craved. I was the Artist, Mentor, Traveller, Leader, Rebel, Stylist and Manger. I could be all of me!

I became very well known in the industry, and my talents were highly sought after. Success came easily and I was thriving, but it wasn't enough. With the success came failures, and I became fixated on the failures. Never satisfied with anything I achieved, nothing was ever good enough. This extended far deeper than perfectionism. The concept of "never enough" was already ingrained in my subconscious mind, and its essence was the driving force behind everything I did or didn't do, for almost 40 years. Personally, it was the force determining why I didn't let people get too close.

By the age of 30, I had shifted into the corporate field, but the same was still true. I excelled in business, negotiations, consulting and team building; but it was never enough. I spent the next ten years studying, honing and refining the art of assertiveness and leadership. I studied human behavior and interaction, and ethical persuasion and influence with one goal in mind: to be good enough.

But on that fateful day, when I was 38, I realized I had failed to achieve my goal, and had failed the one person who meant more to me, than myself—my eldest daughter. For the first ten years of her life, it was just us against the world and we focused on living life to the fullest. I used to tell her that the world gives us enough headaches so we don't invite or create any additional ones unnecessarily. She had been raised in a positive, empowering environment; and together, we were changing the world, one kindness, raised voice, act of dynamic self-expression and giggle at a time.

She was with me through the corporate years when I tried to conform and failed. I was not created to be part of the corporate collective, though I excelled in it. I was built to lead, not to follow.

She and I had moved to Quebec, where I was offered a position working in the heart of the fashion district in Montreal. She attended full French school. A few years later, we moved back to Ontario to open our high-end fashion and consulting boutique, only to lose it after the death of a tenant and over $30 thousand worth of damages he had caused to my property.

This moment in my life was devastating; but it paled in comparison to the day I hit rock bottom.

At the age of 38, we were living in the birth city of my eldest daughter with the father of my second little girl. My baby is only a few months old. The phone rings, at our house, and I answered. The woman on the other end advised me that my eldest daughter was in the hospital and threatening suicide. Time seemed to stop. My only thoughts were, "this must be a mistake; what had I done and how did I allow this to happen?"

I had gone against my deepest knowing. I had gone against my core beliefs. I had committed to a relationship that served to reinstate all of the abuse of my youth. I had silenced my voice for another, and I let go of being the rebel leader, Warrior'ess I was born to be. I let go of being me, and my daughter had witnessed and bared the pain of it all. I had turned my back on myself. I had turned my back on her. How did I allow this to happen?

Her heart was shattered, her disappointment and disapproval was vast. I can still recall the look of contempt in her eyes. I had failed her by failing myself. Now I was the Ghost but, no longer in the Spotlight. I withdrew inside my mind. I was alone.

Mind spinning, too much noise, too much chatter, screaming, make it stop!

Rebirth...

This moment will forever be emblazoned in my mind as the defining moment when everything became faultless. As I was being swallowed up by memories long since buried of rape, abuse and trauma, an overwhelming sense of calm and clarity came over me. The years spent searching for knowledge, studying human behavior, NLP, assertiveness, ethical persuasion and leadership made complete sense now, and had prepped me for this day.

I realized that I actually feared the power contained in my core, and that I had always been "enough". Being born of fire, my alpha, dominant female with a Warrior'ess spirit, who had allowed herself to be supressed by societal norms, was now fully unleashed.

Each one of us has our own story to tell, but they do not define us. We are not victims, martyr's or saints. Our experiences are merely gifts of knowledge sent to guide us to our most powerful existence. We only have to summon our courage.

For me, finding my courage allowed me to create The F.I.E.R.C.E Leadership Formula™. I AM the behind-the-scenes, force of nature, supporting a diverse clientele—struggling with marketing, publicity and ownership of their leadership style—to IGNITE! I AM the Warrior'ess driven to see my clients Thrive in the Spotlight!

Being visible and vulnerable, when introverted, can be difficult initially. However, "if you want to lead the orchestra, then you have to be willing to turn your back on the crowd." With the right tools, right support and right reasons and mindset everything is possible. There are No Limits, as all the World Is a Stage. It's up to us to choose how we shall dance on it!

Renee Mysliwiec, LMT, CHHC, ACADP

Renee Mysliwiec is a holistic health coach, licensed massage therapist, and most importantly, a mother of seven children and "mammy" to 12 grandchildren. She shares her story of how she finally gave herself permission to do what her heart had always yearned. As she found her "gift" through her journey of abandonment, heartache and pain, Renee learned to healed her body, reinvent her life and find her purpose.

Renee is the proud owner of Healing Energies Inc. She specializes in supporting women to transform their bodies, mood, confidence and business; as well as, assisting and empowering them through difficult life transitions. By blending holistic therapies with health coaching, she assists her clients in finding their personal "gift".

🏠 www.healingenergiesinc.com/

✉ renee@healingenergiesinc.com

f www.facebook.com/healingenergiesinc

🐦 www.twitter.com/reneemysliwiec

CHAPTER 27

Discovering My Profound Gift

By Renee Mysliwiec, LMT, CHHC, AADP

෴

I was screaming at the top of my lungs, looking up into the sky and yelling. "WHY? Why did you bring me here so far away from my children and the man that I love? Why Father? Why did you bring me to this godforsaken place?" In the midst of my anguish, I heard the words: *You get a do-over!*

"What, I don't want a do-over!!" Just then, averting my eyes from the road, I realized I was driving past Dixie State College. My mind wandered back to the words. "Really, you mean I could go to school?"

That's what you've wanted, isn't it?

My heart began to race. A flutter of excitement replaced a piece of the deep despair. Could this really be the reason God had sent me here? I took a deep breath as I pulled the car over—my palms sweaty, my heart racing. I had wanted to go back to school for as long as I could remember. I had always felt incomplete without higher education. My heart yearned for school, but there were many reasons for my not going. The kids were so little, acquiring money to pay for college seemed impossible; my husband didn't support the idea, etc.

Now, there was no one to stop me, no little ones to care for and no husband telling me it was too expensive. The decision was left solely up to me. Could I really do this? What if I failed? What if I wasn't smart enough to finish? What if I was the oldest one in the class? These questions swirled in my mind.

I got back on the road and drove to the front of the college and parked. I got out of the car, took a deep breath and braved the walk onto the campus. Immediately, my soul came alive! With the wind whipping my hair and the sun on my cheeks, I felt like a young school girl again. I looked around. There was no one in sight. I took off my shoes and ran down the grassy hill. I wanted to yell, to scream at the top of my lungs, "I get to go to school!! I get to go to school!!" Fear of embarrassment kept me from screaming. I stopped running and decided to look for the administration office. Along the way, a student explained that the office was closed for Spring Break.

OH DARN!

Over the next few days, I contemplated this opportunity which had unexpectedly come my way.

I had been married for 27 years. I married my sweetheart at 19; we started our family six months later. The day I got married was one of the happiest days of my life. Ever since I was a young girl, what I wanted most, in all the world, was to be a mother and a wife. We built a life together and seven beautiful children came from our union.

Marrying so young meant that I had, basically, grown up with the man that I loved so dearly. I didn't know what to do with myself without him. My entire adult life had been devoted to my children and my spouse, but here I was at age 46 living alone—completely alone—without my children or my lover. My life had fallen apart and I didn't know how to pick up the pieces.

My husband had decided that he didn't know who he was anymore. He was having a full-blown mid-life crisis. He was turning 50 and feeling like all his dreams had been unfulfilled. He couldn't find his way out of depression, and he was no longer himself. No matter how much I loved him, or how I tried to help him, nothing seemed to matter. He left in February 2009.

I moved into a smaller house with our three children who still lived at home. Although child support came regularly, it wasn't enough to support us completely. So, for the first time in 27 years, I was a mom working outside the home. I was forced to work three jobs just to get by.

In May 2010 we were told that the home we were renting was being taken by the bank. We moved to a small condo; but a short time after that, I was laid off from all three jobs! I could no longer pay the rent. I was completely beside myself. We were evicted once again.

I found a job in Saint George, 45 minutes from Cedar City. My daughter had offered her home to us, but I knew this had to be a short-term arrangement. Commuting, daily, from Cedar was expensive. I could barely afford the gas. My searches did not produce a house I could afford. My children didn't want to move to Saint George. I knew that even if I found a home, it would be a battle and very hard on them to move. I needed my children to be okay with this. I wanted us to be together.

As a last resort, I spoke with their dad, hoping that he would allow them extended visitation until I could get on my feet. I had also hoped that he'd be willing to continue paying child support, so I could save money for a deposit on another home. He refused. He took the children, but couldn't afford to pay child support and feed them at the same time.

This was the hardest decision of my life. I knew God was drawing me to Saint George, but I didn't want to go. After leaving my children with their dad, I went kicking and screaming all the way. Nevertheless, I was determined. I fully believed it would take just a few months and I'd have a home for us. Little did I know, it would take nine months, my young daughters would never again live with me, and it would be nearly two years before my sons would live in my home again.

Over the course of the next four years, I would have five jobs, earn a degree as a holistic health coach, start my own business and move six times! I was donating plasma twice a week for gas money to drive to Cedar on the weekends to see my children. And although I was grateful for every visit with my family, I was exhausted, struggling with thyroid disease, deeply worried and losing hope.

God knew what I needed. In the midst of my deepest heartache, he had answered my angry screams and showed me this opportunity to go to school. I was able to attend TWO schools at the same time AND have a dear friend as a college room- mate. What an unexpected do-over this was for me!

My journey of education, took me on a path of deep profound personal discoveries. I learned that while devoting myself to my family, over the years, I had somehow lost a piece of my identity. One of my greatest discoveries came during an extreme period of desolation. All I wanted to do was work and make money so that my children could come and live with me, but I kept hitting roadblocks. God kept whispering to my soul: *Give yourself permission to play!*

"There isn't time for play! I'm a grownup. I need to make money. I only have time for survival." I argued.

After four months of no change financially or otherwise, and hearing the continuous pleadings of the spirit, I finally asked in anger, "What the heck am I supposed to do? I am all alone. How am I supposed to play by myself?"

You have a pool don't you?

I stopped dead in my tracks, and had to laugh. "Yes, I have a community pool." I sighed.

The water will be healing. If you will give yourself permission to play, I will teach you how.

This was the day my life began transforming. This was the day I gave in; the day I walked into the healing waters, splashed, yelled, screamed, jumped, kicked, and dove until my heart's content. No one was at the pool. I was alone. It was all mine, and God was teaching me how to play again.

This was the day I gave in; the day I walked into the healing waters, splashed, yelled, screamed, jumped, kicked, and dove to my heart's content. Not just a little part of it, but *every* part; the deepest most secretive parts. He knew my unquenchable desire for knowledge, my love of water; he knew my intense need for the sun. He knew I needed these elements to begin the healing of my heart, body and spirit.

Giving myself permission to attend school and to re-establish playtime gave me perspective and the capacity to reinvent my life, heal my body and my relationships and find my true purpose. I discovered that helping other women through their journey of transformation, healing, and discovery, is my life's work.

In the midst of great pain and sorrow, there is always a gift. Although I came to Saint George reluctantly, this move—away from everyone I loved—brought me to a place of peace, happiness, reconnection and the greatest gift of all: **rediscovering ME.**

Lisa Beane, CHHC, AADP

Lisa Beane, board certified holistic health coach—accredited with the American Association of Drugless Practitioners and The State University of New York—graduated from the Institute for Integrative Nutrition, NYC. Lisa is the founder and CEO of BeaneNATURAL, LLC. She bridges the gap between traditional medicine and holistic health via lifestyle intervention. Her approach incorporates integrative nutrition, bio-individuality and primary foods. Lisa's passion is to empower women to become the healthiest, happiest and best versions of themselves.

Virtual/live retreats, workshops, speaking engagements, published author are among Lisa's suite.

✉ lisa@beanenatural.com

f www.facebook.com/lisa.a.beane

f www.facebook.com/Beanenatural

⌂ http://beanenatural.com

CHAPTER 28

Blessing in Disguise

By Lisa Beane, CHHC, AADP

✃⁄⑥⑥✺

It occurred to me that this lifestyle was silently killing me. It wasn't just the career, though. We liked to live on the edge a little. We made thirteen moves in seventeen years of marriage. I was up for every opportunity that came knocking at our door. The challenge was exciting. The gypsy in me loved this life we created, as it silently and slowly robbed me of life's force.

The frequent overnight travel for work had to stop. The pain my body experienced, the stress of the job and my life, in general, made me vulnerable. I was exhausted beyond measure. As glamorous as it appeared to travel on business, my soul was crying for the craziness to end. I was lonely and living in a hotel room most weeknights, in a bed that wasn't my own. I once discovered the hotel staff had entered my room during the day to deliver flowers and a signed card wishing me a Happy Birthday from them, my hotel family. As grateful as I was for the surprise and their thoughtfulness, all I really wanted was to be at home celebrating with my *real* family. How considerate of the staff to locate my room next to the vending machine so I could take care of my sugar addiction.

March of 2000, an event took place that would shake my world upside down. Hearing the words, *your mom has been rushed to the hospital* and *your mom is gone*, are some of the most terrifying and heart-wrenching words a woman can ever hear. I hung up the phone and fell into Brian's arms crying uncontrollably. The wind had just been taken from my sail. I felt as if the blood had suddenly been drained from my veins and I couldn't stop shaking. Sometime soon after the funeral, I heard the words spoken, *be careful, take care of yourself, you have always been the strong one.*

It was time to venture back home and be with my family after our two-week separation. These two weeks were challenging and draining. I had 250 miles of road to be silent and just "be". It proved to be most depressing. There was emptiness in the center of my gut that made me feel numb and cold. Staring at the road seemingly on autopilot, my thoughts had vanished. Music didn't matter. I had lost part of my soul and my brain was vacant.

As if the car ride wasn't difficult enough, you could hear a pin drop in my home as the sun dazzled through the windows, beautifully bouncing off the lake with a sense of peace and calm. Much to my surprise, returning home to an empty house, tears began to flow with sadness and sorrow. I did not expect this overwhelm of emotion. Home was where it all began and it had now come full circle. I felt lifeless.

Lisa, I don't know why you are still feeling so bad. You are on the best medications there are. The words were deafening to me. My doctor had told me this over and over again, three visits in a row. The words made my heart sink every time I heard them. It was as if a light bulb had gone off and I took his words as meaning, *within my realm of knowledge, I no longer know what to do for you.* My body was crying for help and he didn't know what to do.

I am convinced these words were God's way of speaking to me while channelling through the doctor. I had better listen and take action. I had a wave that came over me. It was a feeling as if there was something more, something deeper, something that I was missing. I realized I was going to have to take my health into my own hands. I also realized that all the drugs, research, medical books, knowledge and wisdom of the best doctors and specialists were not going to fix my health issues.

Arriving back home, I grabbed a garbage bag and threw away every prescription drug that I was on—allergy meds, inhalers, pain meds,

177

steroids, antibiotics, muscle relaxants, nasal sprays, cough meds, anti-inflammatories, anti-yeast & fungal. My health had gone to hell in a hand basket and I was the last to realize it.

Ultimately, I quit my 10-year career to regain my health. I took some time off to rest up, learn to get healthy and get back to work soon thereafter.

It had been a year since I quit. Doctors and specialists were unable to help me. Tears streaming in defeat, it was apparent that I needed to find a better way. I had to find an alternative that would allow me to do the work. So, I prayed:

> *Dear God, please put me into the path of the right people who can teach me to do the work. I am 46 years old, a wife and a mother, and I want my life back. I need your help finding these people and I also need your help finding my way. Please show me the way. I am ready and up for the challenge. In Your name, Amen!*

It is now time to hold on tight to your hat, girlfriend. The people that showed up in my life and the messages that came to me through God and the Universe were indescribable. Some of the messages I received were so far-fetched in my mind that my husband had to get in my face and say, "Why are you resisting? This could be your answer. Traditional medicine has failed you."

Reluctantly, I allowed a non-traditional practitioner to test me. The results were Greek to me. Even though my 10-year career was in Medical Records, I had not seen test results like this. The information I obtained on our call was different lingo than I knew. Among many chronic health issues, I was 100 percent vitamin and mineral deficient, due to a condition called leaky gut. I also had systemic candida.

The doctor was convinced that due to the high yeast count, I contracted candida in the birth canal of my mother when she delivered me. She explained that the candida moved throughout my body, and had formed a fungus in my lungs. She also mentioned that my body was full of toxins, chemicals, viruses, fungus and bacteria. And very confidently she said, "If you don't do something about your health, you have one foot in the grave."

Was this a life sentence? My head was spinning. What did any of this mean? All I'd heard, loud and clear, was that I had one foot in the grave. Period. The end. These quite powerful and gut wrenching words had been spoken. Their force was unexpected and it hit me like a ton of bricks. I was having difficulty understanding what to make of these utterances.

After spending a few moments pondering, it came to me. My dear, sweet mother had lost her life at the age of 66. Was I living a repeat of her life? Before passing away, she had had a majority of the same symptoms; pain, chronic cough and fatigue that now ailed me. The fatigue had taken the wind from her sail, as well. And, she had had a cough for as long as I could remember. I was 37 when she passed away, and I was turning into her. I now had the same chronic cough and had been suffering for approximately twelve years. It acted and sounded just like the cough my mom had.

In my research, I discovered that a fungus in one's lungs could be fatal to a person with a compromised immune system. There is no doubt in my mind that my mom's immune system was compromised. I am saddened by the thought that mom's ill-health went unnoticed. I am crushed to think that had I known then what I know now, maybe her life could have been spared. It is disheartening to say her doctors didn't know what they didn't know.

What an awesome journey I have been on! It has included many avenues towards healing. I decided to open my mind to a variety of modalities, all of which I believe played a significant role in my healing. I am grateful for each and every one of these modalities and would do them all over again.

Blessing in Disguise was born when I was asked to share my story. I truly believe that my mom's premature passing was my "blessing in disguise." I am blessed with improved health and the knowledge that came from many pathways. As a result, I entered school at age 50 to become a Holistic Health Coach. I now empower women; teaching the importance of lifestyle change and maintaining optimal health.

Many blessings and love,

Lisa

Suzanne Hanna, LCSW-R, HHC

Suzanne Hanna is a licensed psychotherapist, holistic health practitioner, spiritual coach, writer and inspirational speaker. She has helped hundreds of men and women move through their fear and pain as a way to live a more inspired life. Suzanne is the co-founder of *The Wilderness Walk*, an experiential journey through the darkness and fear of the inner mind and the pain of the wounded heart in order to help others integrate all aspects of their being, both light and dark. She hosts a popular live, weekly radio show and has a vlog called *InspiredTV*, which highlights leaders who have transformed their pain into purpose.

- www.facebook.com/suzannehannafanpage
- www.thewildernesswalk.com
- www.suzannehanna.com
- www.twitter.com/Suzanne_Hanna
- www.pinterest.com/suzannehanna

CHAPTER 29

Emerging from the Wilderness

By Suzanne Hanna, LCSW-R, HHC

I was hopelessly lost. In just one moment, the beautiful, magical, sweet-smelling forest, that had been my sacred refuge for healing, quickly turned into my worst nightmare. Every tree, plant, bush and rock suddenly became something that could harbour the thing that could lead to my undoing. My golden retriever, Grace, and I had already hiked numerous miles into the dense 517,000 acres of the Allegheny National Forest in western Pennsylvania, since embarking from the trailhead early that morning. There had been various "warning signs" along the trail that told me I should turn back, but I ignored them. Due to several days of rain, parts of the trail had been washed out, making it difficult to navigate and stay on course. How many times have I ignored the signs before? Isn't that what got me on this trail in the first place?

It seemed like only weeks before—instead of a year—I sat lying in bed staring at the ceiling. I was in a very unhealthy relationship but didn't leave because of an intense fear of being alone. In fact, since I'd been eighteen, I had never been alone, and had gone from one relationship to the next as a way to avoid it.

I felt lost and numb after months of being judged and criticized for who I was and what I looked like. I had begun to believe what I was being told. I wanted to run, but my body felt chained to the bed. I felt like a shell of myself—existing, not living; dying a slow and painful emotional death. I wanted more, but I was so afraid to take it! The ironic part was that I was a therapist. I guided people every day with their challenges, moving them effectively out of what wasn't working for them and into what was. I felt like a complete fraud. I knew in that moment that if I didn't leave I would die.

I looked down at the dog we shared, a yellow lab named Henry, and the idea of leaving felt heart-wrenching. I loved that dog. But, I also knew that I couldn't stay for a dog, so I got out of bed and made a radical decision: I would get a dog of my own. It would help me gather the courage to leave.

A couple of weeks later, when the time came to pick up my new dog, I was excited and anxious—excited to meet my new companion, but anxious, too, because taking him home meant really having to leave. I was soon told that there was a problem; the pup had been born with a birth defect and had had to be put to sleep. I dissolved into tears, as I'd pinned all of my hopes on this dog. The woman who handled the dogs seemed at a loss for what to do, but then told me that she had another puppy whose intended owners couldn't take her. Would I be willing to see her as an alternative option?

I was desperate, so I agreed.

Within moments, she brought out this tiny pile of caramel-colored fur with two pink and white gingham bows on her ears. She was placed in my arms; and as I stared into her liquid, chocolate-brown eyes, my heart melted. As I drove us both home, I knew she had been a gift of *grace* and I never doubted what to name her.

From that day on, my healing process began. Three months had passed since that rock-bottom epiphany in the bedroom and Grace was giving me the strength to finally leave. I had told myself that day that I just needed "20 seconds of insane courage" to walk out the door. With Grace beside me, I took those twenty seconds and began the journey of *finding myself*.

Every day, Grace and I hiked in the preserve near my house. There were a lot of tears shed on those trails, with Grace loyally romping by my side. One particular spring day in May, I watched her as she leaped through a field of tall grasses and wildflowers. She was happy and free. I yearned to feel what she felt. I wanted to live so fully in the moment as she was. That very day, I went home, pulled out an atlas, and made the decision to travel. I made a conscious choice to face my greatest fear: the fear of being alone. So, with NO itinerary, we set out.

Most people thought I was crazy, and maybe I was; but for whatever reason, it felt right. I made a commitment to myself that I NO longer would live my life in that paralyzing fear. I knew the only way to do that was to face fear head on. So each day that I hiked, I broke open and wilfully shed all of the defenses that kept me frightened and hidden. I listened to the endless chatter in my brain. I prayed. I cried. I climbed and kept climbing, even when I wanted to give up. I confronted the fragility and uncertainty of myself, and of life, with every moment in the woods.

Now here I was, in one of those uncertain moments, lost and alone as I had been in my relationship just a year earlier. I didn't know which direction would lead me back to the trailhead and out of the Pennsylvania woods. The sun was slowly starting to set and I began to panic as I looked frantically, in vain, for the trail markers that would show me the way back. I knew that I had only an hour or so left of daylight, no food left in my pack and less than a bottle of water. Desperation crept in and fear was coursing through my veins. How would I survive a night in the wilderness with no provisions?

I was quickly brought back to the present when I noticed that not more than 50 yards away was one of my worst fears. A VERY large black bear. I realized that Grace had already taken notice by her alert ears and penetrating stare. The bear appeared preoccupied, as if it was searching for something, possibly food. I knew black bears were omnivores; however, I wasn't sure if this one was hungry enough that an 80-pound dog or a 120-pound human might seem like a viable option. I feared Grace would lunge in order to protect me or bark alarming the bear and compelling him to attack out of self-defense. Instead, she laid down and continued to keep her eyes fervently on the bear. She was quiet as a mouse.

By this time tears were streaming down my face out of intense fear, desperation and hopelessness. Not only was I lost, but now I might be mangled by a bear and left to bleed to death. The thought of witnessing Grace's demise was almost more unbearable. So, I did the only thing I knew I could do in such a moment; I dropped to my knees and began to pray. I prayed as I had done while lying in that bed a year earlier. I prayed for guidance, strength and courage. I prayed for a sign that would show me the way out of the dark wilderness and into the light of my internal knowing. Within moments, from our surrendered state, Grace and I watched as the bear slowly meandered off between the massive trees and soon became hidden by the lush, verdant vegetation of the forest floor.

I felt weak and tired, spent from hours of hiking and emotional exhaustion. I wanted to curl up next to Grace's warmth, nestle into her fur and go to sleep, but the descending sun reminded me that very soon I would be swallowed up by the intense darkness of night. That is when, from somewhere deep within me, I heard the words *keep walking*. I didn't move. I then heard it again, this time louder and more urgent. Grace got up and started to walk towards a very large patch of ferns that glistened from the early evening moisture. She stopped and stared at me as if she was willing me to get up. Although every bone and muscle inside of me screamed with pain and fatigue, I followed her and I started to walk. With each step I felt more determined to find my way out. Within fifteen minutes, we came upon a wooden sign that stated that we were less than a mile from the trailhead.

As I walked toward the light of the trailhead, I saw clearly how the deep woods mirrored the wilderness within me; the fear and pain around my buried and unchartered wounds. With every step I felt freer. I emerged from the wilderness with a greater knowing, more resilience, a deeper faith and abundant gratitude for being led out of the dark.

Sweigh Emily Spilkin, PhD (cand.)

Sweigh Emily Spilkin, PhD (cand.) is a Somatic therapist, Healer for Healers, and a Threshold Guide. She offers programs for healers ready to heal themselves, claim their soul medicine and step into the full embodiment of who they are. She is currently working on her PhD in Post Traumatic Growth. In her free time (yes, that exists!), Sweigh practices radical self-care, romps in the woods of Boulder, CO where she lives and spends time with her community of wild, truth-telling friends. Sweigh can be found on the web at www.ThresholdsHealing.com.

CHAPTER 30

The Path of Initiation

By Sweigh Emily Spilkin, PhD (cand.)

It wasn't a pursuit, so much, my path to the Divine, more like a hunt. Which sounds romantic, except I was the one being hunted.

♦ ♦ ♦

The best stories are the ones that have a question at their heart, not an answer. A

question we can live into. A visceral, red, beating question that pumps through our veins and changes the course of our lives. This is one of those stories.

In 2003, my life fell apart. I was kidnapped, the way Persephone was kidnapped, into the Underworld.

Or was she? I like to think that she had a bit of the temptress in her, that she courted her fate, instead being haplessly taken down. But perhaps I'm getting ahead of myself.

I was competing my stint as the director of an arts program for teens in Boulder, CO, and decided to create a show for the kids in a prominent gallery as my last hurrah.

The show was called "Inside/Out." Each of the teens was given a small cabinet box to embellish in a way that represented their inner and outer lives.

I made a box alongside the kids. The interior of mine was velvety red, with bones and feathers and poems on the walls, and melted wax, and a tree branch growing up through the ceiling.

On the back of the box I attached a pair of splayed wings from a dead pigeon I discovered on the pavement outside the art studio with its rib cage torn open and its bloody heart exposed.

The pigeon should have been a clue. It was the first in a series of dead birds to appear in my life.

I remember the day when I first heard the question. I was in the studio with the kids working on my box.

I decided that I wanted to put a portrait that a friend had sketched of me years before of the front of the box to represent my face to the world. It was fierce and stark and I loved it. But the front of the box had doors so in order to attach the drawing, I would have to cut it in two.

I thought it was no big deal, when I took out the scissors and snipped. What happened next took me by surprise. I started to shake, then hyperventilate, then sob uncontrollably.

The sobbing was a premonition: my life was about to split apart. Only I didn't know it then. I only knew that I was in a room full of teenagers who I was supposed to be leading, with snot running down my nose.

One of the assistants, an art-therapist named Molly, approached and stood behind me as I sobbed. She knew something powerful was happening, and like all good healers, she knew not to stop it. Instead, she assessed the situation and asked one question, a question that would change my life:

"What can happen now that couldn't happen before?"

Not, "Why did you do it?" Or, "What's wrong?" Or, "How can we fix the picture, or the problem, or you?" But, "What can happen now that couldn't happen before?"

When applied to big suffering—like trauma, loss, or illness—that which I was about to enter into—this becomes an essential question. A question that takes an enormous amount of trust to answer. And a willingness to lean into our pain instead of away from it, and to assume that everything, even the things that break us, are doorways to Source, to our own souls, and to what we are here on the planet to do.

"What can happen now that couldn't happen before?"

This is the central question in what is known in academia as Post Traumatic Growth, and what is known in mystic circles as the Dark Night of the Soul, or what I call, the Path of Initiation. Where who we thought we were is dismembered, so that who we really are, naked and more essential, can emerge.

It wasn't a pursuit, my path to the Divine, more like a hunt. Or a fall.

A week after the gallery show I found myself in the desert praying.

I loved directing the arts program, but I knew there was something deeper calling. Even though I didn't know what it was, I had no choice but to listen. So I quit my job and headed for a vision quest in the desert to find out.

I discovered the second dead bird on the first day of the quest, a red-tailed hawk. I sat with its body for three days as I prayed to find my particular way of belonging to the world. I watched as the maggots ate its flesh. And I asked the wind and moon and unseen world: "What is it that is mine to do?"

On the third day, I heard a response: "You must die to who you have been."

Because my longing to become myself was louder then my fear, and because I was blind as to what would happen next, I said yes. Perhaps we have to be blind when we step into the mystery, because if we could see the future, we might refuse our calling.

So I went out on the land and enacted a burial ceremony. I let go of my identity—daughter, writer, program director, artist, friend—burying the old roles in the desert floor. Then I spoke a eulogy and wept.

I went to sleep that night unsure of what I had done, and dreamt of the Southern Cross. I was told to orient to it, that it would show me the way. In the dream, I was standing amongst ancient ruins looking up at the night sky.

A few months later I was in Peru, at Machu Picchu at night, doing a ceremony, staring up at the stars.

I traveled in Peru for two months. I thought I'd receive a message there about my purpose. Barring that, I thought that I'd have an adventure and return to Boulder and open my practice as a healer, something I had been training to do.

Instead, I returned with a parasite that would plunge me into my true healer's training ground.

The chemical sensitivities from the parasite began a month after I returned. At first they were mild, then alarming. After a while, I lost total ability to detoxify the chemicals that are a part of everyday life. The fragrances in shampoos and perfumes, or the compounds in carpets, furniture, and paints would overwhelm my nervous system and cause me to have panic attacks. I had no choice to but drop out of society. My world became unbearably small.

I spent four years nearly housebound determined to find my way through. I read everything I could about healing, grieved, raged, and leaned on friends and family for support. I practiced several hours a day of meditation, detoxed, healed my nervous system, changed my diet, took every supplement known to man, and eventually, with grace, began to heal.

But the true healing was deeper then symptom relief. I learned to find faith in the midst of impossibility. To retrain my brain to focus on what was working instead of what wasn't. To feel deep compassion for myself and others.

At first I felt betrayed by the Divine and by own soul for taking me under. But I learned how to evolve my concept of the Divine from a punishment and reward model to something infinitely more beautiful. I learned how to meet reality on its own terms. To accept life even when

I hated it. And to discover, throughout it all, how radically loved I am. In the darkness, I fell in love with the true face of the Divine. I let my pain break me open to god.

Like many who walk the Path of Initiation, when I was well enough, I studied that which had helped me heal and offered it to others as my service in the world. I became a somatic psychotherapist, a soul guide, and a mentor for other healers on the path.

It wasn't what I would have chosen, or what I thought I was praying for. It was what chose me, what I was built for, my particular way of belonging to the world.

◆ ◆ ◆

A few years ago, the spiritual teacher Ram Dass had a major stroke. When he woke in the hospital, opened his eyes, and realized what had happened, he asked one question: "What grace is this?"

Not, "Why did this happen?" Or "What can I do to get out of it?" But "What grace is this?"

"What can happen now that couldn't happen before?"

These are questions that can change our lives.

◆ ◆ ◆

It wasn't a pursuit so much, my path to the Divine, more like a hunt. Or a fall. Or an alchemical process that transformed my heart, from what I wanted it to be to what it truly is.

Conclusion

Our life stories are the most powerful way to connect with and inspire one another. They represent who we are and what our purpose is here in the world. *In Pursuit of the Divine* will give you hope, courage, faith and strength as you navigate the tidal waves of your life and discover the essence of who you are. In times of adversity, we must commit to knowing and honoring our truth. There is always a gift awaiting us on the other side. The challenge is to silence the mind so you can hear the whispers of your soul. It is within your greatest challenges that lie your most innate inner wisdom, where your soul reveals the next step and you'll witness empowerment.

Now more than ever, women have a burning desire to come together as a collective to support, guide, nurture, fiercely love and cultivate our Feminine Power. You're invited to join our circle of women on your own quest in pursuit of the Divine. The Feminine Rising is the world's leading community and sanctuary for empowering a women's soul.

Feminine Rising Sanctuary

In Pursuit of the Divine is calling all women who have a deep desire to come together and join forces within the Feminine Rising Community. Open to the magic of life's offerings with harmony and flow and regain your feminine power. The Feminine Rising is the world's leading community of healing retreats for empowering a woman's soul. Each member of our sacred circle has a unique offering to guide you on a healing journey. Experience a nothing held back love and support as you step in and explore, open, embody and deepen the relationship with yourself, and every element of your life, in service to your true freedom. This is for the rising Feminine who yearns to be seen, heard and acknowledged for who she is as she returns to her worthiness, wholeness and true essence. Uncover the depths of your purpose through your own powerful story. Discover your own inner wisdom and strength as you dive deep into the Feminine within.

"When the Feminine rises, she cultivates love from the depths of her soul, she becomes a gift to the world."

http://femininerisingretreat.com

The End